Quod scriptura, non iubet vetat

The Latin translates, "What is not commanded in scripture, is forbidden:'

On the Cover: Baptists rejoice to hold in common with other evangelicals the main principles of the orthodox Christian faith. However, there are points of difference and these differences are significant. In fact, because these differences arise out of God's revealed will, they are of vital importance. Hence, the barriers of separation between Baptists and others can hardly be considered a trifling matter. To suppose that Baptists are kept apart solely by their views on Baptism or the Lord's Supper is a regrettable misunderstanding. Baptists hold views which distinguish them from Catholics, Congregationalists, Episcopalians, Lutherans, Methodists, Pentecostals, and Presbyterians, and the differences are so great as not only to justify, but to demand, the separate denominational existence of Baptists. Some people think Baptists ought not teach and emphasize their differences but as E.J. Forrester stated in 1893, "Any denomination that has views which justify its separate existence, is bound to promulgate those views. If those views are of sufficient importance to justify a separate existence, they are important enough to create a duty for their promulgation ... the very same reasons which justify the separate existence of any denomination make it the duty of that denomination to teach the distinctive doctrines upon which its separate existence rests." If Baptists have a right to a separate denominational life, it is their duty to propagate their distinctive principles, without which their separate life cannot be justified or maintained.

Many among today's professing Baptists have an agenda to revise the Baptist distinctives and redefine what it means to be a Baptist. Others don't understand why it even matters. The books being reproduced in the *Baptist Distinctives Series* are republished in order that Baptists from the past may state, explain and defend the primary Baptist distinctives as they understood them. It is hoped that this Series will provide a more thorough historical perspective on what it means to be distinctively Baptist.

The Lord Jesus Christ asked, *"And why call ye me, Lord, Lord, and do not the things which I say?"* (Luke 6:46). The immediate context surrounding this question explains what it means to be a true disciple of Christ. Addressing the same issue, Christ's question is meant to show that a confession of discipleship to the Lord Jesus Christ is inconsistent and untrue if it is not accompanied with a corresponding submission to His authoritative commands. Christ's question teaches us that a true recognition of His authority as Lord inevitably includes a submission to the authority of His Word. Hence, with this question Christ has made it forever impossible to separate His authority as King from the authority of His Word. These two principles—the authority of Christ as King and the authority of His Word—are the two most fundamental Baptist distinctives. The first gives rise to the second and out of these two all the other Baptist distinctives emanate. As F.M. lams wrote in 1894, "Loyalty to Christ as King, manifesting itself in a constant and unswerving obedience to His will as revealed in His written Word, is the real source of all the Baptist distinctives:' In the search for the *primary* Baptist distinctive many have settled on the Lordship of Christ as the most basic distinctive. Strangely, in doing this, some have attempted to separate Christ's Lordship from the authority of Scripture, as if you could embrace Christ's authority without submitting to what He commanded. However, while Christ's Lordship and Kingly authority can be isolated and considered essentially for discussion's sake, we see from Christ's own words in Luke 6:46 that His Lordship is really inseparable from His Word and, with regard to real Christian discipleship, there can be no practical submission to the one without a practical submission to the other.

In the symbol above the Kingly Crown and the Open Bible represent the inseparable truths of Christ's Kingly and Biblical authority. The Crown and Bible graphics are supplemented by three Bible verses (Ecclesiastes 8:4, Matthew 28:18-20, and Luke 6:46) that reiterate and reinforce the inextricable connection between the authority of Christ as King and the authority of His Word. The truths symbolized by these components are further emphasized by the Latin quotation - *quod scriptura, non iubet vetat*— *i.e.,* "What is not commanded in scripture, is forbidden:' This Latin quote has been considered historically as a summary statement of the regulative principle of Scripture. Together these various symbolic components converge to exhibit the two most foundational Baptist Distinctives out of which all the other Baptist Distinctives arise. Consequently, we have chosen this composite symbol as a logo to represent the primary truths set forth in the *Baptist Distinctives Series.*

A
Sober Discourse
of
Right
to
Church-Communion

WILLIAM KIFFIN, A.M.
1616-1701

A
SOBER DISCOURSE
of
Right
to
CHURCH-COMMUNION

By

William Kiffin A.M.

*With a Biographical Sketch of the Author
by John Franklin Jones*

LONDON: 1681

he Baptist Standard Bearer, Inc.
NUMBER ONE IRON OAKS DRIVE • PARIS, ARKANSAS 72855

Thou hast given a *standard* to them that fear thee;
that it may be displayed because of the truth.
– *Psalm 60:4*

Reprinted 2006

by

THE BAPTIST STANDARD BEARER, INC.
No. 1 Iron Oaks Drive
Paris, Arkansas 72855
(479) 963-3831

THE WALDENSIAN EMBLEM
lux lucet in tenebris
"The Light Shineth in the Darkness"

ISBN# 1579782396

TABLE OF CONTENTS

	Page
Introduction	11
TO THE CHRISTIAN READER	13
THE PREFACE	19
CHAPTER ONE: *The Question Stated*	25
CHAPTER TWO: *Reasons Why Unbaptized Members May Not Be Admitted to the Lord's Supper*	29
CHAPTER THREE: *Shews that this Practice of Admitting Unbaptized Persons to the Lord's Supper, is Against Scripture*	39
CHAPTER FOUR: *Shewing that this Opinion that Unbaptized Persons May Be Admitted to the Lord's Supper, is Against the Practice of All Christians in All Ages that have Owned Ordinances*	51
To *Illustrate this Point* Further We Will Give a Brief	59

Abstract of Some Things Recorded in that Excellent History Compiled by the Divines of Madeburg.

CHAPTER FIVE: Wherein the *Objections Against this Position* viz., that None May be Regularly Admitted to the Lord's Supper, that are not First Baptized, *are Answered.* 75

A BIOGRAPHICAL SKETCH OF WILLIAM KIFFIN (1616-1701) BY JOHN FRANKLIN JONES 97

A
Sober Discourse
OF
Right
TO
Church-Communion.

Wherein is proved by *Scripture*, the Example of the *Primitive* Times, and the Practice of All that have Professed the *Christian Religion:* That no Unbaptized person may be Regularly admitted to the *Lord's Supper.*

By *W. Kiffin* a lover of Truth and Peace

Act 2. 41. *Then they that gladly received His Word were baptized: and the same day there were added to them about three thousand souls.*

Deut. 5. 32. *Ye shall observe to do therefore as the Lord your God hath commanded you; you shall not turn aside to the right hand or to the left.*

Col. 2. 5. *Joying and beholding your order and the stedfastness of your faith in Christ.*

London, Printed by *Geo. Larkin,* for *Enoch Prosser;* at the *Rose* and *Crown* in *Sweethings-Alley,* at the East End of the *Royal Exchange,* 1681.

TO THE
CHRISTIAN READER

When it pleased God of His free grace to cause me to make a serious inquiry after Jesus Christ, and to give me some taste of His pardoning love, the sense of which did engage my heart with desires to be obedient to His will in all things, I used all endeavors both by converse with such as were able, and also by diligently searching the Scriptures, with earnest desires of God, that I might be directed in a right way of worship; and after some time concluded that the safest way was to follow the footsteps of the flock (namely that order laid down by Christ and His Apostles, and practiced by the primitive Christians in their times) which I found to be that after conversion they were baptized, added to the church, and continued in the apostles' doctrine, fellowship, breaking of bread, and prayer; according to which I thought myself bound to be conformable, and having continued in the profession of the same for these forty years, although through many weaknesses, and fears, temptations, and sufferings, yet not without some witness from God of His gracious acceptance and strength to this very day: The sense I have of my own weakness and inability, would have been a bar to me to appear in this public way, did I not see a necessity lying upon me for the Truth's sake, and the sakes of many, by reason of some that have lately risen up to weaken, if not make void, that great ordinance of baptism, by endeavoring to maintain that all persons that believe, although they never did, nor do practice the same, may partake of the ordinance of the Lord's Supper, and all other Gospel instituted duties. A notion, not only contrary to the primitive pattern, but the constant practice of all that ever professed the Christian religion, or that own the Scriptures to be the Rule of Faith and Practice; and it would be a happiness to the Christian religion, if all that profess the same, did in other things agree as they do in this; namely, that none ought to be partakers of the Lord's Supper but such as have been baptized; those that differ in this matter from them, would be found to be as few in number as they are weak in argument, and although I am well satisfied that the performance of all duties and ordinances, will be of no value to any man, further than Christ is enjoyed in them: the very Gospel itself severed from Christ, will prove the administration of death (2 Cor. 1:21). The most powerful preaching, and the clearest discourse of the free grace of God hath no life in it, unless the soul be led by the Spirit to Christ, Who is the life of all duties. Knowledge of the Truth, and obedience to it in outward performances, will as little save a man's soul as the covenant of works. Yet every man that hath an interest in Christ, is bound by the Word of God to be obedient to all His commands. It was the great commendation of Zacharias and Elizabeth, that they walked in all the commandments and ordinances of the Lord blameless, the ordinance of baptism is none of the least, the very foundation of religion being comprehended in the form thereof, as appeareth at large by the worthy and learned Dr. Owen, in his book of the Divine Nature and Personality of the Holy Spirit, page 50, viz., All things necessary to this purpose are comprised in the solemn form of our initiation into Covenant with God (Matt. 28:19). Our Lord Jesus Christ commands His Apostles to disciple all nations, baptizing them in the name of the Father, and of the Son and the Holy Ghost. This is the foundation we lay of our obedience and profession, which are to be regulated by this initial engagement, page 51. No sense can be affixed unto these words but what doth unavoidably include His personality, we are alike baptized into Their Name, equally submitting to Their authority, and equally taking the profession of Their Name upon us. Again, by being baptized into the name of the Father, and of the Son and of the Holy Ghost, we are sacredly initiated, and consecrated, or dedicated unto the service and worship of the Father, Son and Holy Ghost; this we take upon us in our baptism: herein lies the foundation of all our faith and profession with that engagement of ourselves unto God, which constitutes our Christianity; this is the pledge of our entrance into Covenant with God, and of our giving up ourselves unto Him in the solemn bond of religion. And concludes in page 52. If the Doctrine of a Trinity of Persons subsisting in the same undivided essence, be not taught and declared in these words, we may justly despair of ever having any Divine mystery manifested unto us. I leave the reader to peruse it at large.

If this ordinance of baptism be the pledge of our entrance into Covenant with God, and of the giving up ourselves unto Him in the solemn bond of religion, and we are hereby dedicated unto the service of the Father, Son, and Holy Ghost, then must it of necessity be the first ordinance, before that of the Lord's Supper. We may as well conclude a man may go into a house before he enters, and a man may be paid for his goods, and afterwards receive earnest, as any may lawfully partake of the Lord's Supper before he is baptized. And if we are sacredly initiated and consecrated, or dedicated unto the worship of the Father, Son, and Holy Ghost as that text Matthew 28:19 sheweth we are, and take this upon us in our baptism, and thereby owning the Spirit to be God, equal with the Father, and the Son, as that faith which is to be exercised by us in all other ordinances, then the admitting of persons to the Lord's Supper, and other instituted duties, before they are baptized, doth greatly weaken this main argument of the Spirit's being God, at least in the practice of these Gospel duties, for from what Scripture will be made appear, that He is so to be owned in them, if ye partake of them before, or without being baptized? If this be laid as the foundation of all our faith, and profession, which are to be built upon in all our profession, if it be omitted, the structure must needs be weak, we had need rather to have our faith strengthened in the belief of so great and essential a Truth as the Divine essence of the Spirit is, by the use of all means

appointed to that end.

To the Christian Reader

Mr. Francis Cheynel, in his learned treatise, of the Divine Trinity, printed 1650, page 258, quotes it as the judgment of Iraeneus, Tertullian, Athanasius, Basil, and others of the ancients, that the principle fundamentals of the Christian faith are contained in the form of baptism, and founded on Matthew 28:19. And in page 185 tells us, if any man in Athanasius' time asked, how many persons subsist in the Godhead, they were wont to send him to Jordan, and there you may hear and see the blessed Trinity. Matthew 3:16, in page 381. God the Holy Ghost is to be obeyed, we are devoted and consecrated to the belief, worship and service of God the Father, God the Son and God the Holy Ghost. By which we may see, what esteem the ancients had of that ordinance, and great reason there is for every Christian to be found in the practice thereof, seeing they are thereby baptized into Father, Son and Holy Ghost, as the first foundation of our visible profession of Christ; for as repentance is the visible initiating grace; so baptism is called the baptism of repentance as the first initiating ordinance.

I have for the satisfaction of all, endeavored in the following essay to clear this truth both from Scripture and example, as also to produce the judgment of the learned in all ages. As for our modern divines, you have their own words set down faithfully by me, and as for those who are more ancient, I have requested a friend to translate the same, which I doubt not but is done impartially. And although I may expect to meet with censures from some who will be ready to charge the truth herein with uncharitableness and to be of a dividing nature; yet I can with comfort and sincerity of heart in the presence of God declare, I have no other design, but the preserving the Ordinances of Christ, in their purity and order as they are left unto us in the holy Scriptures of Truth; and to warn the churches to keep close to the rule, lest they being found not to worship the Lord according to His prescribed order he make a breach amongst them, neither are you presented with any new opinion, but that which hath been the judgment of all that have professed the Christian religion in all times; so that what censure any shall make upon it, respects not us only, but the servants of God of all persuasions in all ages, and for myself, as I have a witness in my own conscience, so I doubt not but I have the same also with those that know me, that I have made it a great part of my duty, as I have had opportunity, to persuade all Christians to love and peace, to avoid judging, and reproaching each other under their differing persuasions, to turn their hearts and passions, which hath greatly abounded in our days one against another, into prayer, and supplication for another, that although they differ in their light, it may not make any breach in their love; He that knows most of the mind of God, knows but in part, for who art thou that judgest another man's servant? I shall trouble you no further, but leave the perusal of this small essay to thy serious consideration.

Thine in the service of Christ,

W. K.

THE PREFACE

What was praiseworthy in those primitive Christians, to whom the Apostle Paul writes (1 Cor. 11:2), can be no blemish, but really a duty in other Christians, in after times, to imitate; his words are, I praise you, brethren, that ye remember me in all things, and keep the ordinances as I delivered them to you: our translation of the Greek word (rendering it "ordinances") is excepted against by some Papists, especially Gregory Martin, reputed a great linguist in the Rhemish Seminary, who would have it translated (traditions) to countenance the Romish opinion; to which shall be opposed that the Greek word signifies indeed tradition, that is in English, a delivery, viz. of doctrines, ordinances, instructions, or institutions (2 Thess. 2:15), by those evangelical preachers to their auditors, which is nothing else but the Doctrine of the Gospel first preached (which is of the greatest and highest authority,) and afterwards committed to writing by the evangelists and apostles, as standing records to future ages; so that any traditions, besides what is written, are justly to be excepted against, and (in matters relating to Divine worship) to be esteemed apocryphal. Because a delivery of transactions or doctrines by ancestors to posterity by word of mouth, is liable to many mistakes and uncertainties, by reason of the different constitutions and circumstances of men, who frequently introduce that authority to color their inventions, or the product of their imaginary fancies, with respect to Divine matters. Though it is very apparent that such a rule is not at all self-evidencing, for it cannot prove itself; nor is it demonstrative, for it has no certain medium to convince; nor universally true in all times and places, because reports vary everywhere; neither is it unerring, being nowhere stamped with that character; and lastly, not plain, for no doubting person can possibly examine all traditions. Now these are some of the properties of a general rule to try controversies by, which being wanting in oral traditions, the word cannot here be understood otherwise than by ordinances or institutions of the Gospel recorded in the Scriptures, which were given for our instruction (2 Tim. 3:16), written by the immediate dictates of the Spirit; preserved by the gracious Providence of God in the church from the injuries of time, ignorance, and fraud, through all ages; they have been kept with much greater care, than any other books, translated into all languages, retained both by orthodox and heretics, diligently observing and watching each other, so that there could not possible happen any remarkable variation or alteration in them, but that presently the whole world would have exclaimed against it.

Man's nature is very prone to be medling with things beyond his commission, which has proved the very pest and bane of Christianity; for notwithstanding that dreadful prohibition (Rev. 22:18, 19) of adding to, or taking from His Word, is not Europe full of pernicious additions and subtractions in the worship of God, which are imposed as magisterially as if enstamped with a Divine character, though in themselves no other than (as Christ Himself calls them) the traditions of men (Matt. 15:3)! It is a superlative and desperate piece of audacity for men to presume to mend anything in the worship of God; for it supposes the All-wise Lawgiver capable of error, and the attempter wiser than his Maker. And if sovereign princes and worldly states be so jealous of their prerogatives and respective rights, that they will (to the utmost hazard) repel any invader: if men be displeased to have their laws undervalued by the private judgments of those who rather interpret than obey them: if the conquest of an enemy against the command of his general, cost a Roman gentleman his life, though his own father were the judge: if the killing of a lion contrary to the laws of the King's hunting (though to rescue the King himself) cost a poor Persian his head: if the architect that brought not the same (but as he judged, a fitter) piece of timber than he was commanded, to a Roman consul, was rewarded with a bundle of rods. If (Lev. 10:1, 2) Nadab and Abihu came to a tragic end for their prohibited service, in offering not the same that was commanded, but strange fire before the Lord; what shall we say to such as mix their inventions with the sacred institutions and prescripts of the great unerring Sovereign? When the same person who is to perform the obedience, shall dare to appoint the laws? Implying a peremptory purpose of no further observance than may consist with the allowance of his own judgment? Whereas true obedience must be grounded on the majesty of that power that commands, not on the judgment of the subject, or benefit of the prescript proposed; not so much from the quality of things commanded, as from the authority of him that institutes. Is not such a practice an invasion upon Christ's prerogative? Do not such men make themselves (as it were) joint authors of His ordinances? And may it not be truly said that whoever practices any institution otherwise than as was appointed by the Supreme Lawgiver, does not honor the ordinance, but an idol of his own making? Mixtures are useful for two purposes; viz. Either to slacken and abate some thing that is excessive, or to supply something that is deficient: and so all heterogenous mixtures do plainly intimate, either a viciousness to be corrected, or a defect to be supplied. Now it is no less than blasphemy to charge either of these upon the pure and perfect Word of God, and any glosses that take away or diminish the force of it, or human traditions that argue any defect, are equally dangerous and impious. To stamp anything of a human original with a Divine character, and father it upon God, is one of the highest and most daring presumptions the pride of man can aspire unto, and is provided against by special prohibitions and threatening (Deut. 12:32 and 18:20; Jer. 26:2; Prov. 30:6).

When that question shall be asked, Who hath required this at your hands? I doubt it will be no sufficient plea to say, that if we have erred in any punctilio's of Divine Truth, it was for peace and unions sake, etc. For, no motions of peace are to be made or received with the loss of Truth: nor may the laws, orders, and prescriptions of Christ be altered or varied, in any tittle, upon any pretense whatsoever, God having never given any such prerogative to mankind, as to be arbitrators how He may be best and most decently worshipped.

It is not to be questioned but all protestants, or any sober impartial persons, that bear any reverence to the Divine Majesty and His Holy Word, will readily own these general theories, which are so self-evidencing, that if any gainsay them, he does at the same time strike at the Majesty, Wisdom and Authority of GOD, the most daring and desperate enterprise in the world.

Now this being (as it must be) granted, viz. That no part of God's law, or worship, whether we respect the manner or form, or the matter and substance thereof, is to be altered without the express order and direction of GOD Himself; it will lead us to a sober inquiry, Whether the opinion here examined, be grounded upon the Law and Word of God. To do which, for method's sake,

Chapter 1 We will state the question.

Chapter 2 We will propose some reasons why unbaptized persons may not be admitted to the Lord's Supper.

Chapter 3 We will produce some Scripture demonstrations to evidence that such a practice (viz. so to admit them) is not evangelical.

Chapter 4 We will shew that it is against the practice and judgment of all Christians that have owned ordinances, for above sixteen hundred years.

Chapter 5 We will answer objections.

In the prosecution of which heads, we shall labor to sift out Truth impartially, propose our own judgment candidly and plainly, without the least reflection upon, or prejudice to our Christian brethren that dissent from us in this point, with whom and with all that can own the name of the Lord Jesus according to his Gospel, we desire to live in brotherly love and Christian society, and if we find our brethren entertain any unsound notion with respect to Gospel Truths, we look upon it as our duty to endeavor to inform them of it, in a meek and sober way; and if we fail of success, then to leave them to the Lord, who in His own due season will uncloud those sacred mysteries, which yet are hidden to a great many.

We are not willing to be censorious, nor arrogate that wisdom to ourselves, as to think that we are wiser than others, yet in all modesty we may be bold to affirm, that in the point here handled, we have the Scriptures, and the concurrence (see Chapter 4 following) of all Christians from the beginning, to this age, on our side; whereas the opposite opinion can challenge but a few favorites, and is of a very late original: which is not the main reason brought here to oppose it, but only serves for a collateral evidence, to illustrate the arguments proposed from Scripture, and to shew that the eminent professors of, and sufferers for, Christianity have owned it, which is no slight circumstance to sober and considering Christians.

Chapter One
The *Question* Stated

*A Sober Discourse
of right to church communion:
wherein is proved,
that no unbaptized person
may be regularly admitted to
the Lord's Supper, etc.*

In the stating of this question, it may be necessary to examine how far we disagree, and wherein we concur with our dissenting brethren, because that will prevent much needless discourse, and lead us to debate the matter in dispute only.

The professors of the Christian religion are distinguished by certain terms, invented by their opposites, to know them by, as Prelatical, Presbyterian, Independent, Anabaptist, etc. And it were well if such names were laid aside, and the Title of Christian brother reassumed, because they agree in fundamentals. Now of all these, our controversy in the case in hand is only with some of the last, who are (though not rightly) called Anabaptists. As for the others, their avowed principle is, to admit none into church-fellowship or communion, that are unbaptized: yea so positive are the Papists, that they look upon all so far from being qualified for church communion, till they are baptized, that they say they are all damned that die without it; but we derive no authority from their practice. The Church of England receives no member into their communion without baptism, neither do Presbyterians, Independents, nor, indeed, any sort of Christians that own ordinances, admit any as a church-member without baptism. We shall therefore direct this discourse to our dissenting brethren, of the baptized way only, who reason thus: that there being no precept, precedent nor example in all the Scripture, for our excluding our holy brethren that differ in this point from us, therefore we ought not to dare to do it.

Now how unsafe, unsound, and of what pernicious consequence, such a position in its direct tendency is and has been, shall appear in the chapter of Objections; to which as present we refer — Only in general we say, that if by precept, precedent, or example, is meant such, in express words, viz., such texts of Scripture as prohibit practices by name and circumstance, then Popish Purgatory, and monkery and ten thousand other things, as Doctor Owen well says, may be made lawful by this argument, there being not an express word in Scripture that prohibits those things by their very name, because not then in being. If it be meant what may be inferred by direct and plain consequence in the true logical notion of it, without sophistry or quibble, I am satisfied we can produce precept, precedent, and example, that it is our duty to withdraw from disorderly walkers. And our dissenting brethren grant, that the administration of baptism, by rantism or sprinkling in infancy is disorderly, as being a practice without example or consequent warrant from Scripture, and administered to a subject not capable, or qualified to receive it, nor in an orderly manner. And therefore it is so much the more wonderful, that they above any, should blame us for obeying the solemn command we read, viz., "Now we command you, brethren, in the name of our Lord Jesus Christ, that ye withdraw yourselves from every brother that walketh disorderly, and not after the tradition which ye received of us," (2 Thess. 3:6), which last phrase, "the tradition which ye received of us" (the word *Paradosis* signifying not only Doctrine delivered, Matt. 15:2,3, but also a command, ordinance or institution, as

The Question Stated

before, 2 Thess. 2:15) plainly makes out that they were not only to withdraw from persons of disorderly conversation, or defective in morals, but also from such as were corrupt in doctrine, or disorderly in their gospel administrations, that being as great a violation of gospel order, and as pernicious to Christians as immorality, which must be granted, or else there is no authority given to the church to deal with members of corrupt principles, etc.

Now this command being general, includes all disorders of any kind, in manners, doctrine, or practice, and is sufficient warrant (were there no more) for our obedience, to exclude such as disorderly practice the ordinance of baptism, from our immediate communion at the Lord's table, though not from our love and affection, for we hope they walk according to their light, and the error being not so fundamental as to endanger their eternal state, we esteem them Christian brethren and saints, for whose further illumination we daily put up our prayers.

But in regard we are convinced (1) That it is the duty of all believers to be baptized in water upon confession of their faith, etc. (2) That none but such ought to be baptized. (3) That such as practice otherwise deviate from the rule of the Gospel, and the precedents recorded there. (4) That such a deviation is in itself disorderly, and in the consequence dangerous, as bringing many unregenerate members into the church, etc. We conceive ourselves bound by the indispensable rule of our duty, to bear our testimony against such a practice, and in the most healing manner we can, to discharge ourselves from being countenancers, or abettors of it, which we can do no other way (unless they will be reclaimed) than by withdrawing from those disorders; after the example of the primitive saints, of the ancient Waldenses, our modern Reformers, etc. (5) We are satisfied that we are guilty of no schism in that particular, for we separate not from any Christian as such, but hold communion as far as we agree, and where we cannot agree, we dare not but obey the command before recited, though we expose ourselves to worldly inconveniencies by it; the least particle of Divine Truth being more valuable than anything the world can present: for which our brethren should not blame us, but rather seriously examine our reasons and arguments, and then judge.

The farther prosecution of this matter is referred to its proper head: and therefore we shall propose to consideration the following inquiry, viz.

QUESTION: Whether persons unbaptized may regularly be admitted to the Communion of the Lord's Supper?

To obviate a cavil, which may be made, the reader may understand that under the term [unbaptized] we comprehend all persons that either were never baptized at all, or such as have been (as they call it) christened or baptized (more properly sprinkled) in their infancy. Now our dissenting brethren with whom we have to do, look upon this way to be absolutely invalid, and so no baptism (else they would not be baptized themselves) and consequently esteem all such as unbaptized: so that we need not prove what is granted; and shall therefore proceed to examine the question in the following chapter.

Chapter Two

Reasons Why Unbaptized Members May Not Be Admitted to the Lord's Supper

That persons unbaptized may regularly be admitted to the Communion of the Lord's Supper, is denied from these reasons:

1. Because this opinion tends to destroy the nature, ends and uses of these Gospel ordinances. The nature of baptism is spiritual, when rightly administered: was it not sumitted unto by the primitive Christians? Was it not the first act done by them after their conversions (Acts 2:41,42)? Whereby they became visible professors of the Gospel of Truth, which figured their death, burial, and resurrection with Christ (Rom. 6:4, Col. 2:12). Is it not an institution stamped with as divine a character, and as sacred a sanction as any in Scripture? All nations taught, being to receive it, and being of the same duration with preaching, submitted to by Christ Himself, before He entered upon His public ministry (which is the most illustrious example in the world) witnessed unto by the renowned worthies of all ages.

Now that this ordinance being of that quality, enforced by so great authority, submitted to by such examples, and serving for such gracious ends (as to be the symbol of regeneration, in which a believer is made a partaker of those divine conveyances, those communications of grace, and increasings of faith, promised by the Lord Jesus to His sincere followers) should be put in danger of being quite abolished, and the practice lost by an unseasonable and mistaken apprehension, and that by such persons as own baptism to be as here represented, is a matter something strange, and 'tis to be feared, will prove in the consequence of ill effect, not only to this, but the succeeding generation, if they that espouse it should go about to propagate this new principle: to prevent which, (if it may please the Divine Will to bless these lines) was the only end of this essay, and that purely out of the zeal I have to preserve (as much as in me lies) the ordinances in their purity, as they were delivered to us by Christ; for we all know what a vast trouble and hazard the Reformers (and indeed many that are alive at present) had to rescue this, as well as other truths and ordinances, from the ridiculous additions of sanguinary persecuting Romanists, under whose captivity it groaned for some ages.

To enforce what is said, I shall endeavor to shew here some of the ill consequences of this opinion, and the small reason our brethren have to propagate it, though I still reserve much to the chapter of Objections, where their reasons will be more largely replied to.

1. This opinion has a direct tendency to invalidate, or indeed, quite throw out of doors, and discontinue the use of a foundation ordinance, or principles of the Gospel of Christ (Heb. 6:2). For if unbaptized persons may be admitted to all church privileges, does not such a practice plainly suppose that it is unnecessary? For to what purpose is it to be baptized (may one reason with himself) if he may enjoy all church privileges without it (Supra sit per plura quod fieri potest perpinciora)? The Baptists (if once such a belief prevails) would be easily tempted to lay aside that reproached practice, (which envious men have unjustly derided and aspersed) of being dipped, that is baptized, and challenge their church communion by virtue of their faith only; and such as baptized infants would be satisfied to discontinue the practice, when once they are persuaded, that

their children may be regular church members without it; for if it be superfluous, discreet and thrifty people would willingly be rid of the trouble of Christening feasts (as they call them) and all the appurtenances thereto belonging: so that in a short time we should have neither old nor young baptized, and by consequence be in a likely condition to lose one of the Sacraments, which would easily make way for the loss of the other, both having an equal sanction in Scripture; and the arguments that disannul the one, will destroy the other, and consequently all ordinances and modes of worship, and lastly, religion itself. For if a thing expressly commanded and practiced by Christ, be looked upon as unnecessary, every man will conclude, that 'tis all one, whether he takes or leaves it, and will, if he can choose, rather leave it, since the taking it up, is something troublesome and of no use (as is supposed) which begets an opinion, that Christ's Laws may be dispensed withal by men, and so lessens that reverence and esteem which persons ought to have for Christ: and when such do once make a breach in those boundaries and limits, which they are enjoined not to pass, they seldom stop in that extravagant career till they run beyond all religion into Atheism, or pretended Enthusiasm. So that (at best) this opinion tends to encourage persons in the neglect or contempt of religious duty, or to the loss thereof quite and clean; which is, no less, than to be, not only an accessory, but (in a great measure) the cause of that sin.

2. This opinion gives up a cause and truth that has been by judicious pens well defended both from Scripture and antiquity, and which these brethren themselves are convinced to be a Gospel Truth: for if it be once admitted that it is not necessary to church communion, every man of sense will infer, that our contentions for it were frivolous, our separation schismatical, and our suffering the penalties of human laws, foolish: and consequently, we shall be exposed to the reproaches of such as are (without this advantage) ready enough to revile and persecute us.

3. This opinion perverts, or rather destroys order and flatly

Reasons Why Unbaptized Members May Not Be Admitted to the Lord's Supper

contradicts the practice of the primitive Christians; it is said, "Then they that gladly received His word were baptized" (Acts 2:41). Here is the right Gospel order. First, they that gladly received the word; that is, they that believed, and no other, were immediately baptized (that it was immediately appears by the adverb then) which was the second work, and the same day (viz., after they believed and were baptized) "there were added unto them (that is, received into church-fellowship, by faith and baptism) about three thousand souls. And they continued steadfastly in the Apostles' doctrine and fellowship" (that is, in the same faith and communion) "and in breaking of bread and prayers" Acts 2:42, (that is, in the enjoyment and administration of church ordinances). Is not here a famous instance or precedent of their practice, which answers those frequent and indecent clamors of such who call for Scripture to justify the exclusion of our holy brethren that have not been so baptized (2 Thess. 3:6). Whereas in the foregoing pages, there is a Scripture cited, that justifies our withdrawing from disorderly walkers; and such as make this outcry own the practices of infant baptism in that particular to be such, and therefore our separation for that reason (pursuant to that express command) lawful; which they must grant, or deny infant baptism to be disorderly; or else must say, that there be some disorderly walkers, that we may and ought to have communion with, notwithstanding that solemn prohibition of it (2 Thess. 3:6).

And whereas it is said, that baptism was never ordained of God to be a wall of division, between the holy and the holy; the holy that are, and the holy that are not so baptized with water, as we, etc. It is answered.

1. The phrase [wall of division] is ambiguous; if it be meant of a total exclusion of other Christians from our love, charity, and Christian communion, as far as we agree; we do not look upon baptism to be such a wall of division, neither do we so practice it.

2. If it be meant, of an excluding from immediate church-

fellowship, although we meet not with this phrase [viz., wall of division] in those very words, yet we find what is equivalent in 2 Thess. 3:6 and several other texts: and it is remarkable, that the word translated disorderly (ex a priv. and Ordinatus inordinatus vel ex ordine, out of Order) is a **metaphor** borrowed from the custom of war, wherein every soldier hath his station assigned him, from which, when he swerves, he becomes disorderly, which the Apostle elegantly uses, to denote that every Christian is a soldier that's listed under the banner of Christ, and must keep his exact station appointed him, without the least inclining to the right or left hand, backward or forward, without the word of command. Beza upon the place tells us, that Livius was wont to use this word of soldiers, that kept not their station: and Stephanus call those soldiers by this name, who are disorderly. From this emphasis of the word, we may gather that if military commanders expect a punctual and regular obedience from their soldiers; and severely punish such as break their array, or quit their stations; the Lord (who is a jealous God with respect to His worship, and positive institutions) will call any, that presume to break the order He had prescribed, to a severe account, as hath been, and shall be, further demonstrated.

3. This assertion reaches any other gospel-ordinance, as well as baptism: for if it should be said, that the Supper was never ordained of God to be a wall of division between the holy and the holy, that do not so receive it as we, it will as rationally follow with respect to this, as well as baptism, that we should not exclude a person that doubts it, or positively asserts it to be needless, from our communion, which may be likewise said of any church ordinance whatsoever; and consequently, the Rule of Communion must not be what we find written, but the sanctity of the party (whether pretended or real) that proposes himself as a member. For I would ask those that pretend tenderness, and for that cause admit persons to the Lord's Supper that are unbaptized, that if any person should desire to join to a church, and yet declares, he wants light to practice the ordinance of the

Reasons Why Unbaptized Members May Not Be Admitted to the Lord's Supper

Supper, but in other things would be of their communion, whether they would admit him upon those terms, he wanting light in that ordinance of Christ wherein the communion of the church doth chiefly consist? If they would admit him, they open so wide a gap, that any ordinance upon the like pretence may be dispensed with, and two or three, yea all, as well as one, may be cashiered, and church order may be quite turned to an anarchy. If they would not admit a person upon the said terms, then 'tis necessary to produce some Divine Law that makes the Supper more essential than baptism, or else the practice can never be justified. But that no such authority can be shewn, is undeniable; for the Divine Law that ordained the supper, did also establish baptism. If it be said "Take eat, this is my body. This do in remembrance of me," (Matt. 26:26; Luke 22:19; 1 Cor. 11:24), etc., it is also said, "Go teach all nations, baptizing them in the name of the Father, and of the Son and Holy Ghost" (Matt. 28:19); "Repent and be baptized every one of you for the remission of sins," (Acts 2:38) etc.; "Arise and be baptized and wash away thy sins," (Acts 22:16) etc.

Do the former Scriptures institute the Supper, and command its constant observation? The latter do as well institute baptism and command its constant observation, the very same sanction, the same Spirit, with equal authority establishes both, giving baptism precedency in order of time, as being the sacrament of the spiritual birth, and the other of spiritual nourishment and growth; and surely there is as much need of being new born, as being spiritually fed, that being of absolute necessity with respect to priority in order to this.

Did Christ Himself celebrate this Supper, as before? Why, the same Lord Jesus, before He entered upon His public ministry, was baptized, "And Jesus when He was baptized, went up straightway out of the water; and lo, the heavens were opened to him, and he saw the Spirit of God descending like a dove, and lighting upon Him; saying, this is my beloved Son, in whom I am well pleased." (Matt. 3:16, 17). Here the whole Trinity appears, the Father by a voice, the

Reasons Why Unbaptized Members May Not Be Admitted to the Lord's Supper

Son in His body, and the Holy Ghost like a dove: all three make the triumph, and ratify the affair; never was any ordinance graced with such a presence, nor made authentic by a more illustrious example.

Does the Supper shew forth the Lord's death till He come? (1 Cor. 11:26). So baptism is a lively symbol of the death, burial and resurrection of Christ (Rom. 6:4; Col. 2:12).

Does examination go before the Supper? (1 Cor. 11:28). So faith and repentance, the two great Gospel graces, with confession of sins, are necessary antecedents to baptism (Acts 2:38; 8:37), and all these are altogether as necessary before the Supper.

Is it said, "Whoso eateth my flesh and drinketh my blood, hath eternal life"? (John 6:54), etc. So it is said, "He that believeth and is baptized shall be saved," (Mark 16:16), etc.; "The like figure whereunto, even baptism doth also now save us not the putting away the filth of the flesh, but the stipulation (or answer of a good conscience toward God, by the resurrection of Jesus Christ." (1 Pet. 3:2 1). As the Supper is a spiritual participation of the body and blood of Christ by faith, and so (not merely by the work done) is a means of salvation; so baptism signs and seals our salvation to us which lies in justification and discharge of sin, etc.

By this brief parallel we may see that baptism is not only ordained and ratified by the great Lawgiver, as well as the Supper, but that it is dignified with as spiritual encomiums as any Gospel ordinance can be; and if the advantage inclines to either of them, it is evident that the New Testament more frequently mentions the command and practice of baptism than of the Supper: for besides the Great Commission (Matt. 28:19; Mark 16:15,16; etc.), you have frequent precepts and examples of it (Acts 2:38; 8:38; 9:18; 10:48; 16:15, 33; 18:8; etc.). Neither do we find any one ordinance of the New Testament so made use of by the apostle to incite Christians to die to sin and live to God, as this ordinance of baptism, being that which is signified thereby is called a burial with Christ (Rom. 6:4); a putting on of Christ (Gal. 3:27); the signification of the washing away of our sins by the blood of Christ (Acts 22:16); that having an interest in Christ, and being buried with him, "We may walk in newness of life," etc. Whereas besides the institution of the Lord's Supper by Jesus Christ, instanced by the several evangelists, that ordinance is but four times mentioned, viz. Acts 2:42, 20:7, 1 Cor. 10:16 and 11:23 by all which it appears that the ordinance of baptism, as it has the precedency in point of order, so it is more frequently mentioned, and more earnestly inculcated, than the other, and therefore the obligation to preserve it, as delivered by Christ and His Apostles is indispensable.

4. In regard it is granted by such as hold the opinion here argued against, that baptism and the Supper, etc., are positive institutions it will unavoidably follow, that all the force and authority they have upon the conscience in point of practice, is to be derived from the plain express Law and Word of God, which made them ordinances; from whence only we are to seek both a warrant for, and the method and manner of practicing them. The direction given to Moses was, "See that thou make ALL things according to the PATTERN shewed thee in the Mount" (Heb. 8:5; Ex. 25:9-40). And no less exact are Christians to be in the administration of Gospel ordinances; since to deviate from the express rule, is branded with the odious title of will-worship and human tradition.

All sound and orthodox writers with one mind agree (and mere reason teaches it) that where a rule and express law is prescribed to men, that very prescription is an express prohibition of the contrary: here we have the order of gospel administration, not only commanded, but practiced (Acts 2:38-42). First they preached; and such as were converted, were baptized; such as were baptized, walked in church-fellowship, etc., breaking of bread and prayers; which being so express, what necessity is there to be wise above what is written, and to clamor for precept or example, to prove that baptism is a bar to communion, since we read everywhere

Reasons Why Unbaptized Members May Not Be Admitted to the Lord's Supper

(where Gospel order is set down) that all such as were received, were first baptized; and not one instance in the whole Bible, that any were received without it. Nor is it rational to think that any were admitted to church fellowship any other way, unless we will say that these positive precepts were calculated for some only, and not for all Christians, which is not only absurd, but against the very letter of the Scripture, "Teach all nations, baptizing them," (Matt. 28:19), that is every individual that gladly receives the Word in every nation: "Take eat, etc. Drink ye all of it" (Matt. 26:26), etc. That is, every individual member of the church. Which interpretation must needs stand, until the maintainers of this new opinion can assign to what sort of Christians these Divine precepts are obligatory, and to what sort they are not; a thing impossible to be made out. Which I shall shut up in the words of Mr. Coxe, in his late <u>Discourse of the Covenants,</u> page 131. "In matters of positive right (sayeth he) we can have no warrant for our practice, but from a positive precept: for things of this kind fall not within the compass of common light, or general principles of natural religion; but have their original from a particular, distinct, and independent Will of the Lawgiver. And therefore inferences built upon general notions may soon lead us into mistakes about them; if upon such inferences we form a rule to ourselves of larger extent than the express words of the institution do warrant." Which as it is a sound and excellent truth, quite overthrows this practice of admitting unbaptized persons to the communion of the Lord's Supper, there being no positive precept to warrant it: and therefore is queried (Quere how consistent, etc.) how this, their opinion can be consistent, or reconciled with these expressions?

To conclude: The ends and uses of baptism being (1) to represent to the eye and understanding by a visible sign or figure what hath been preached to the ear and heart; (2) to witness repentance (Matt. 3:6,11; Acts 2:38; Mark 1:4); (3) to evidence regeneration, called in allusion to it the washing of regeneration (Titus 3:5); a being born of the water

Reasons Why Unbaptized Members May Not
Be Admitted to the Lord's Supper

and the Spirit (John 3:5); (4) a symbol of our dying unto sin, and living again to Christian newness of life (Rom. 6:4; Col. 2:12; etc.) It is therefore an ordinance of very great significance, and such as go about to lay it aside (as this opinion in its tendency and consequence must needs do) deserve no thanks from the churches of Christ, who have experienced much of the Lord's presence in its regular and orderly administration.

Chapter Three

Shews that this Practice of *Admitting Unbaptized Persons* to the Lord's Supper, *Is Against Scripture.*

To demonstrate this truth we shall add some further enforcements from that text before-mentioned, viz. 1 Cor. 11:2. "Now I praise you brethren, that ye remember me in all things, and keep the ordinances as I delivered them unto you."

The Apostle having in the foregoing chapter, verse 14, exhorted them to fly from idolatry, shewing the great danger of mixture in the worship of God, in verse 22, brings them to consider the danger; "Do we provoke the Lord to jealousy? Are we stronger than He?" And verse 23 to prevent all mistakes sheweth that in things of an indifferent nature, there might be a lawful use of them provided therein all occasion of offense were avoided. And elsewhere (viz. Rom. 14), he treats largely of the duty of saints to bear one with another, and not to withdraw their love and affections from each other, where the matter of difference lay only in such things as in themselves had no relation to the worship of God.

In the beginning of this chapter he exhorts them to be followers of him as he was of Christ, by which he informs them that no man's practice or example ought to be any further followed than they follow Christ.

In the text he commends them for their care in keeping the ordinances of Christ pure, both with respect to matter and form, as appears by the phrase [as they were delivered unto

Shews That This Practice of Admitting Unbaptized Persons to the Lord's Supper, is Against Scripture.

you] from whence we may observe,

That it is a practice praiseworthy for the churches of Jesus Christ to preserve and keep the ordinances of Christ, as they have been delivered by Christ and His Apostles to them, because,

1. We hereby advance the wisdom of Jesus Christ, Who has in His house ordered all things so, to the effecting of those ends for which He hath appointed them, that there is no necessity of man's additions, either with respect to the matter of them, or the order and method in which they are disposed. Now the church of Christ is His house, and His wisdom shines greatly, not only in the food He hath provided for them, but in the way by which they receive it from Him, there being nothing that entrenches more upon the wisdom of God, than that (when He hath prescribed a method in His Word) men should presume to alter or change the same; it being a much greater sin than the bare omission of any duty, for by our omissions we shew only our weakness and shortness of what we should know and do; but by additions, we cast a blemish upon the wisdom of Christ, as if we were wiser to order things than He.

That which occasioned so great an astonishment in the Queen of Sheba (1 Kings 10:4,5,8), was the observation of the order of Solomon's house, which made her admire his wisdom. And surely the wisdom of Christ is very eminently seen in the order wherein the ordinances of His house ought to be practiced. The Apostle (Col. 2:5) rejoiced to behold not only the steadfastness of their faith, but their order also in the Gospel of Jesus Christ.

2. Because the ordinances of Christ are given by Him to His people as a trust, and therefore great care and fidelity must be used to keep them as they were delivered by Him: for as in human affairs, the exact conscientious and upright management of a trust, is a certain note of the integrity and honesty of the trustee, so the violation of it is a high breach and violation of sincerity and faithfulness. Hence the Apostle

Shews That This Practice of Admitting Unbaptized Persons to the Lord's Supper, is Against Scripture.

so earnestly exhorts Timothy to "keep that which was committed to his trust" (2 Tim. 6:20). Yea, the glorious Gospel itself (of which this Holy ordinance is a part), is said to be committed to the apostle's trust, (1 Tim. 1:11) and so it is indeed committed to the care and trust of all true churches of Christ, who are to be accountable for it, to the great Lord and author of it, the Lord Jesus Christ, etc.

3. Because it preserves the beauty of the house of God; for whatsoever is prescribed by the Lord Jesus, with respect to His worship, is full of beauty, harmony, and order, everything answering its respective end, and what is signified thereby: and as Grace shines in its lustre in the orderly exercise thereof; so do the ordinances of Christ: for as regeneration is the first work of God upon the soul, in order to the exercise of the graces of Christ given, so hath He appointed baptism, as that which is the first ordinance to be practiced, which doth more particularly, than any other ordinance in the signification of it, hold out, and visibly represent our new birth, and therefore is called the Baptism of Repentance (Mark 1:4; Luke 3:3).

Suitable hereunto does that learned and eminent divine, Mr. Daniel Rogers, express himself (Treatise of the Two Sacraments, p. 71, printed 1633.) "Baptism then is the first sacrament of the Gospel, consisting of water, which is sacramentally Christ; or wherein by water duly applied, not only the presented party is made a member of the visible church; but also sealed up to an invisible union with Christ, and thereby interested in all those benefits of His, which concern the being of Regeneration.

By calling it the first sacrament, I point at the precedency and order of baptism, the which all those names of baptism both in Scripture, and elsewhere, do approve. It's the seed of the church, as the other is of food. It issued first out of the side of our Lord Jesus upon the cross. It's the creating instrument of God to produce and form the Lord Jesus to a New Creature, and to Regeneration in the soul. It's called our union with Christ, our marriage-ring, our military press-money, our

Shews That This Practice of Admitting Unbaptized Persons to the Lord's Supper, is Against Scripture.

matriculation, cognizance and character of Christ, our implanting or engrafting into Him and His body, our ship, our ark, our Red Sea, our putting on of Christ. For as all those go before our nourishment, communion, cohabitation, service, fruit, manna, or food from Heaven, so this sacrament must go before the other. Breeding, begetting and bringing out of the womb, doth not more naturally go before the feeding of the infant by the mother's breasts, than this womb of the youth of the church goes before the milk thereof; the church being no dry nurse, but a mother of her own, the sons and daughters of her own womb — let all who desire to taste of the sealing power of the second sacrament to nourish them as saints first prove the sealing power of the former sacrament to beget and make you saints." And a little after (p. 72), "Beware — lest the Lord be froward with them that fight against the God of Order: lest instead of finding nourishment before breeding, as they rob God of His order, so they meet with wrath and judgment, before mercy and salvation; yea, lest God accurse their single emptiness of Christ, with such a double barrenness, as will admit no conception or birth."

And very pathetically (p. 73), after he hath shewed that Christ hath joined water with a kind of equal necessity with Himself (Mark 16:16; John 3:5), subjoins, "Shall not he who despiseth water (appointed to such an inseparable Holy end) despise the ordainer of water? (Ex. 20:7) Shall we take His name in vain, by slighting that by which He makes Himself and the power of His word and Spirit manifest to beget the soul to Him, and be holden guiltless? (Matt. 19:6) When Christ hath put both in one, shall we dare to say the one is strong, the other is base? Shall we slight it, slack our haste to it, our Holy preparing of ourselves to it, our abiding at it, our offering up prayers for blessing it, our making it the joint object of our humiliation, faith, reverence, and thanks? Far be it from us, so to abhor that Popish hyperbolical esteem of it, and the merit of the work wrought of it; that we run into another riot to disesteem it? Doubtless he that cares not for Christ in the Word, Christ in the promise, Christ in the

Shews That This Practice of Admitting Unbaptized Persons to the Lord's Supper, is Against Scripture.

minister, Christ in the water, Christ in the bread and wine, Christ sacramental; cares as little for Christ God, Christ flesh, Christ Emmanuel. By these He comes near. And 'He that despiseth you, despiseth me, and him that sent me' (Matt. 10:40). Beware we of such contempt, even in the secretest of our thoughts and affections: and let Christ in the water be honored as Christ, for that sweet union and fruit which He brings to poor souls thereby. If Jordan be precious when God will use it, for the angels healing by it, much more this (2 Kings 5:14; John 5:2)." Page 8 1. "The Lord's scope in baptism is an inward grace, but this general privilege is to all equal, viz. a badge of an outward member: distinction from the common rout of the world, out of the pale of the church. The Lord appointed circumcision as a seal of the righteousness of faith chiefly: yet as an overplus he allowed it to be the differencer of all other nations from the Jews. It was a fence and wall of separation from them in all their converse. So is baptism now a mark or badge of external communion: whereby the Lord settles a right upon the person to His ordinances, that he may comfortably use them as his own privilege, and wait for the inward prerogative of saints by them. And yet this (as much as men boast of it) is but a shell in respect of the other." So far he.

Again, baptism holds out the soul's interest in the death, burial, and resurrection of Christ in a more special manner than any other ordinance, it is called the stipulation or answer of a good conscience, by the resurrection of Jesus Christ from the dead (1 Pet. 3:21); that is, when a conscience appeased and pacified with the discharge of sin, can cry, "Abba, Father" with a holy security, and speak to God Himself, etc. Now this stipulation of a good conscience is the effect of baptism, and which baptism seals: for what it finds it seals, although it doth also exhibit more of the same kind. A learned expositor (Mr. Thomas Goodwin), gives his sense of this place thus: "The answer of a good conscience is here attributed to Christ's resurrection, as the thing signified and represented in baptism, and as the cause of that answer of a good conscience, even baptism (sayeth he) doth now save

Shews That This Practice of Admitting Unbaptized Persons to the Lord's Supper, is Against Scripture.

[us] as being the ordinance that seals up salvation, not the putting away the filth of the flesh, or the washing of the outward man; but the answer of a good conscience towards God by the resurrection of Christ from the dead." (To open this, sayeth he) "Our consciences are that principle within us, which are the seat of the guilt of all the sins of the whole man, unto whose court they all come to accuse us, as unto God's deputy, which conscience is called good or evil, as the state of the man is. Now in baptism, forgiveness of sins and justification being sealed up to a believer's faith and conscience under that lively representation of his Communion with Christ in His resurrection; hence this is made the fruit of baptism; that the good conscience of a believer sealed up in baptism, hath wherewithal from thence to answer all accusations of sin that can or do at any time come in upon him, and is, as it is here added (by virtue of the resurrection of Jesus Christ) namely in this respect, that his communion with Christ in His resurrection hath been represented in his baptism as the ground of his faith, and of that answer unto all accusations."

By all which we may (by the way) see of what necessity faith is required of the persons that are baptized, if they will receive any benefit thereby. Also, how baptism being the first ordinance to be administered, answers to the first grace received; from whence it appeareth, that as the grace of regeneration gives a right to the enjoyment of gospel institutions; so baptism, with respect to priority and order, is the first institution, without which, none may regularly partake of other church ordinances.

And this further may be noted as considerable, that as there is but one beginning of natural life to man; and one beginning of spiritual life, which is by regeneration (John 3:3), so baptism is to be but once administered (Ames Medulla Theol. p. 183. "The Supper of the Lord ought oftentimes to be administered to the same person, etc.); whereas, if baptism had the same import and signification with respect to the privileges that are to be enjoyed at the Second Coming of Christ as the Supper of the Lord hath, there would be the same reason for the frequent administration of it, as is for the Supper of the Lord.

4. It is commendable to keep the ordinances of Christ pure, as they were delivered, because it prevents the creeping in of the inventions of men in the worship of God. For (as it was before noted) man is naturally apt to be meddling that way, and mixing something of his own with those sacred institutions which God has with greatest severity prohibited, having not spared any, no not His own people, though what they have done therein seems not to be out of any wicked intentions, but rather out of an ignorant zeal: of which there are many instances in Scripture as before recited; particularly, the memorable cases of Nadab and Abihu (Lev. 10:2,3); Uzzah (2 Sam. 6:6,7), etc.

Suitable hereto, Mr. Burroughs very excellently expresses himself in his book entitled Gospel-Worship, or the Right Manner of Sanctifying the Name of God, pages 8,9, etc.

"All things in God's worship must have a Warrant out of Gods Word, must be Commanded; it's not enough that 'tis not Forbidden, and what hurt is there in it? But it must be Commanded. When we come to Matters of Religion and the worship of God, we must either have a Command, or somewhat out of Gods Word, by some Consequence drawn from some Command, wherein God manifests his Will; either a Direct Command, or by comparing one thing with another, or drawing Consequences plainly from the words, we must have a Warrant for the Worship of God, etc. When any creature is raised in a Religious way above what it hath in it by Nature, if I have not Scripture to warrant me, I am therein Superstitious — We must be all Willing-Worshippers, but not Will-Worshippers, Matth. 15:9. Isa. 29:13.

Page 10. You see how severe God was to Nadab and Abihu, for but taking other Fire then that which God appointed, to offer up Incense, though there was no direct Commandment against it, etc.

Page 11. In the matters of Worship God stands upon little

Shews That This Practice of Admitting Unbaptized Persons to the Lord's Supper, is Against Scripture.

things, such things as seem to be very small and little to us, yet God stands much upon them in the matter of Worship. For there is nothing wherein the Prerogative of God doth more appear, then in Worship, as Princes stand much upon their Prerogatives. — There are — things in the Worship of God that are not written in our hearts, that only depend upon the will of God Revealed in his Word; which were no Duties except they were Revealed there. And these are of such a nature, as we can see no Reason for, but only this, because God will have them. — Though men would think it a little matter whether this Fire, or that Fire, and will not this burn well as that? But God stands upon it. — When Uzzah did but touch the Ark, when it was ready to fall, we would think it no great matter; but one touch of the Ark cost him his life. There is not a minimum in the Worship of God, but God stands mightily upon it. — For a man (Numb. 15:32) to gather a few sticks (on the Sabbath) what great matter was it? But God stands upon it. So when the men of Bethshemesh did but look into the Ark, it cost the Lives of fifty thousand and seventy men, etc.

He further adds, page 12, That there is no privileges or dignities of man, that can secure them from God's stroke; instancing Nadab and Abihu's case, Moses, the man of God being their uncle, and Aaron their father, men newly consecrated to the Priest's office, renowned men that God put much glory upon; yet if they will venture but to offend God in this little thing, His wrath breaks out upon them, and kills them presently, etc.

This eminent servant of God adds much to the same effect in the said book which for brevity is passed over and amongst the rest, offers several reasons by which he judgeth that Nadab and Abihu were good men, and gives a plain demonstration that they had no wicked design, as (1) they were young men, newly come to their office, and might not understand all things, as if they had had longer experience. (2) Its observable for verse 1. 'Tis called strange fire, which he commanded not, that if there be not a command for our practice, nor such a precedent as the Scripture approves of, no human pretense can excuse the transgressor from the judgment of God.

Beza, in his annotations upon the third verse, I will be sanctified, observes that the meaning of it is, I will punish them that serve me otherwise than I have commanded, not sparing the chief, that the people may fear and praise my judgments. There is also a notable instance, I Samuel 6:13, 15, 19, concerning the men of Beshemesh, who being in the field reaping their harvest, rejoiced at its return (vs. 13) and therefore offered sacrifices to the Lord (vs. 15) but because they looked into the ark, fifty thousand, threescore and ten men of them (as was said) were slain. The like instance we have (as was already urged) about Uzzah (2 Sam. 6:6), whom God smites dead for touching the ark, etc.

It is concluded by all Orthodox writers, that the rise of Antichrist was by degrees, first encroaching by one invention, and then from time to time, super-adding another; which is indeed no wonder, for if a church once swerves from the rule in one thing, a foundation is thereby laid of doing so in many things. And for this reason the Apostle with great earnestness charges Timothy, and in him all saints, thus, I give thee charge in the sight of God, etc., that thou keep this commandment without spot, unrebukeable, until the appearing of our Lord Jesus Christ (1 Tim. 6:13,14). The Apostle had in this epistle been instructing Timothy about church worship, and things relating to prayer, eldership, dealing with members, etc., and therefore concludes, I charge thee to keep this commandment; that is, that which he all along in the epistle directed and pressed with so weighty arguments: as if he had said, It is your indispensable duty to be careful in this, because, as 'tis expressed (vs. 15, 16), in his own time he shall shew who is the blessed and only potentate, etc. Jesus Christ hath given gospel-worship to His church, as King of His church: The potentates of the world shew their power in nothing more than in keeping those who are employed by them to the strict observation of the commissions given to them; so that if an ambassador goes beyond his commission, he forfeits his head;

Shews That This Practice of Admitting Unbaptized Persons to the Lord's Supper, is Against Scripture.

and therefore, if anything be demanded, or any particular offered in order to a treaty, which is not in their commission, they usually answer, I have no commission to answer or meddle with this or that point. Now sayeth the Apostle, Keep the commandment blameless without spot: Jesus Christ is King of kings, and Lord of lords, the only Potentate, and in His time he will shew it, and examine by what commission from Him they have done what they have done and practiced, and will ask this great question, Who hath required this at your hands? What satisfactory answer can any man give, if such a thing be allowed? If you ask a rule for baptizing children, may not such a person demand where your rule is for unbaptized persons to receive the Lord's Supper? If you ask a rule for signing with the cross in baptism, he will ask where your rule is for baptizing of children, and in a word, if any one thing be admitted in point of practice, that has not the express warrant of God's word, it will make way for others, because the same reason or pretense that establishes one, may equally be produced for another, and another, without end; and so a deviation from rule in any thing, though never so small, tends directly to bring in the inventions and traditions of men into the worship of God. From the whole of what hath been said, we may infer these corollaries or inferences,

1. That God hath prescribed a particular way and method in which He will be worshipped.

2. That He is so tender and nice therein, that the least variation from His own stated order will not be allowed by Him, which appears by the punishment of such as transgressed, and the praises given to such as kept His ordinances as they were delivered unto them, mentioned at large before.

3. That to swerve from the Lord's institutions, and invert His order, has a direct tendency to destroy all modes of worship, and consequently all the public and solemn exercise of religion, inasmuch as the same reason by which one ordinance may be changed, or discontinued, will equally

prove the change or discontinuance of any, yea, of all at long run.

4. And if the first churches might not be constituted without this ordinance of baptism, neither may those that succeed them, because the same reason that made baptism necessary to them, makes it also necessary to us. For Gospel order settled by Apostical authority and direction, as this was, hath not lost any of its native worth and efficacy, or obliging virtue, by any disuse or discontinuance occasioned by any, but ought to be the same to us now, as it was to them in the beginning of such order; especially considering the day wherein we live, many endeavoring to bring in their own inventions into the worship of God, which should make all Christians be more careful and zealous to cleave to the institutions of Jesus Christ, as they were first delivered by the holy penmen, and the practices of the primitive Christians.

To conclude this head, as baptism is not to be repeated, because it is the sacrament of regeneration, initiation, and incorporation, which are not capable of reiteration, so neither can the seal and sign thereof; so whatsoever makes for the not repeating it in the ordinary use of it, makes also for this as fully or more, that it should be the first.

If it be not to be repeated because it is the sign or seal of initiation, regeneration and incorporation, by the same reason it must be first, as initiation, admission, incorporation, and regeneration are the first internal acts in us, and upon us, by which we are made Christians. But of this we have said enough before.

Chapter Four

Shewing that this Opinion that Unbaptized Persons May Be Admitted to the Lord's Supper, is *Against the Practice of All Christians in All Ages* that have Owned Ordinances.

As for the practice of gospel times, it hath been evidently demonstrated, that the Apostles and disciples of Christ, did constantly baptize such as were converted, and that after they were taught, the next thing was to baptize them, neither durst they break that order, the Scripture rule being, "Teach all nations, and baptize them," (Matt. 28:19); "Make disciples and baptize;" "He that believeth and is baptized, shall be saved" (Mark 16:16) — you see here the rank of baptism immediately; after teaching, after believing, it holds the first place of ordinances properly Christian: Ye may see it again, in the rule in Peter's preaching, "Repent and be baptized" (Acts 2:38), which was instantly put in practice, which is a second head of proof — namely Scripture example, for "they that gladly received his word were presently baptized, to the number of 3,000" (Acts 2:41), after which they continued constantly — in Christian fellowship; and in the practice of ordinances, as the Lord's Supper, prayer, etc. (vs. 42). In the example of the eunuch you have the same, as soon as ever Jesus was preached, and he discovered water, "What hinders me," saith he, "to be baptized?" "Nothing," saith Philip, "if

Shewing that this Opinion that Unbaptized Persons may be Admitted to the Lord's Supper, is *Against the Practice of All Christians in All Ages* that have Owned Ordinances.

thou hast faith," so he was instantly baptized. (Acts 8:38; 10:48). The like ye have of Cornelius, who upon the first preaching of Christ, before the assembly was baptized he and his.

The like you have of the jailor (Acts 16) to whom at midnight (being astonished by a miraculous action) the word was preached, and to all in his house, and he and all his believing, were forthwith all of them baptized. Here was no loss of time, and for the order, it was after faith, and before any other administration. There may be other instances given, but from these and the foregoing pages, this conclusion necessarily follows, that baptism in point of order and time, is the very next ordinance to believing. Not but that there ought to be fit time allowed for the trail of faith, wherein to be sure the Apostles were not negligent, as being an absolute duty.

As it is certain that in the history of the gospel or whatsoever relation we have in the New Testament, as to matter of fact or precepts, in matter of right, relating to the order and administration of baptism, do clearly hold forth the order to be after faith, and the subject baptized by immediate and necessary consequence, an actual believer; so on the other hand it is evident, that there is not the least tittle either in express terms, or rational and plain inference, in the whole New Testament, to countenance the opinion we oppose. (1.) There is no precept directly or consequentially commanding us to receive any member without, (2.) nor one instance to be produced that ever it was done. (3.) It is evident, that the abettors or promoters of such a practice now, do in so much invert God's order, and lay a dangerous foundation for the abolition of this great and sacred institution of our Christian baptism.

As for the ages next to the Apostles, for near 300 years, we have examined the records of those times, and find that the ordinance of baptism was retained by the churches in the same order and mode of administration as is recorded in the

Shewing that this Opinion that Unbaptized Persons may be Admitted to the Lord's Supper, is *Against the Practice of All Christians in All Ages* that have Owned Ordinances

New Testament, viz, first they taught and preached the gospel, then they baptized all such as were so taught, and so immediately received them into the communion of the church.

As to the practice of the second century, we have a memorable instance in Justin Martyr's second apology to Autonius Pius the Roman Emperor, as Mr. Baxter renders it in his Saint's Rest, ch. 8, Section 5, viz.,

"I will declare unto you how we offer up ourselves to God after that we are renewed through Christ, those amongst us that are instructed in the faith and believe that which we teach is true being willing to live according to the same, we do admonish to fast and pray for the forgiveness of sins, and we also fast and pray with them, and when they are brought by us into the water and there as we were NEW BORN (that is baptized) are they also by New Birth (viz. baptism) renewed; and then calling upon God the Father, and the Lord Jesus Christ, and the Holy Spirit they are washed (that is baptized) in water. Then we bring the person thus washed and instructed to the brethren (as they are called) where the assemblies are, that we may pray both for ourselves, and the new illuminated, that we may be found by true doctrine and by good works worthy observers and keepers of the commandments, and that we may attain eternal life and salvation. Then bread and wine being brought to the Chief Brother (so they call the Chief Minister) he taketh it and offereth praise and thanksgiving to the Father, by the name of the Son and Holy Spirit, and so a while he celebrateth thanksgiving. After prayer and thanksgiving, the whole assembly saith, Amen.

Thanksgiving being ended by the President (or Chief Guide) and the consent of the whole people the deacons, as we call them, do give unto every one present part of the bread and wine, over which thanks was given, and they also suffer them to bring it to the absent.

This food we call the Eucharist, to which NO MAN is admitted, but only he that believeth in the truth of the doctrine, being washed in the laver of regeneration for

> Shewing that this Opinion that Unbaptized Persons may be Admitted to the Lord's Supper, is *Against the Practice of All Christians in All Ages* that have Owned Ordinances.

remission of sins, and that so liveth as Christ hath taught."

So far this learned Father and martyr gives a positive account of matter of fact in his time from whom we may plainly be informed that no unbaptized person was then admitted to the Lord's Supper.

Dr. Cave in his <u>Primitive Christianity,</u> page 296, part 1, chap. 10.3, Edition printed 1676 says thus, "Our Lord having instituted baptism and the Lord's Supper as the two great sacraments of the Christian Law, they have accordingly been ever accounted principal parts of public worship in the Christian church — baptism is the door, by which persons enter in, and the great and solemn rite of our initiation into the faith of Christ, etc.

The persons by whom this sacrament was administered, were the ministers of the gospel, the stewards of the mysteries of Christ, baptizing and preaching the gospel, being joined together by our Savior in the same commission, etc.

"Nor was it accounted enough by some in these times that baptism was conferred by a person called to the ministry, unless he was also orthodox in the faith — hence sprang that famous controversy between Cyprian and Stephen, Bishop of Rome, concerning the rebaptizing those that had been baptized by heretics, Cyprian asserting that they ought to be rebaptized, etc., calling a council at Carthage of 87 African bishops, who all concluded for his opinion — for they looked upon that baptism that had been conferred by heretics as null and invalid (seeing heretics being out of the church, could not give what they had not) and therefore when they returned to the union of the church, they could not properly be said to be rebaptized, seeing they did not receive what (lawfully) they had not before, etc."

Then, p. 305, after he had discoursed of infant baptism, adds that "those who made up the main body of the baptized in those days were adult persons, who flocking over daily to the

Shewing that this Opinion that Unbaptized Persons may be Admitted to the Lord's Supper, is *Against the Practice of All Christians in All Ages* that have Owned Ordinances

faith of Christ, were received in at this door. Usually they were for some considerable time catechized and trained up in the principle of the Christian faith, till having given testimony of their proficiency in knowledge ... and of a sober and regular conversation, they then became candidates for baptism, and were accordingly taken in, etc.

Page 308. "Persons finding themselves at any time surprised with a dangerous or mortal sickness and not daring to pass into another world without this badge of their initiation into Christ, they presently signified their earnest desire to be baptized, which was done accordingly as well as the circumstances of a sick bed would permit. These were called Clinici of whom there is a frequent mention in the ancient writers of the church, because baptized as they lay along in their beds. This was accounted a less solemn and perfect kind of baptism, partly because 'twas not done by immersion, but by sprinkling, etc.

Page 333. "The persons communicating at this sacrament (viz., the Lord's Supper) were at first the whole church or body of Christians within such a space, that had embraced the doctrine of the gospel, and been baptized into the faith of Christ, used constantly to meet together at the Lord's table. As Christians multiplied, and more exact discipline became necessary, NONE were admitted to this ordinance, till they had arrived at the degree of the faithful, for whoever were in the state of the catechumens under instruction in order to their baptism, or by reason of any heinous crime under the censures and suspension of the church, and not yet passed through the several stages of the penitents, might not communicate, and were therefore commanded to depart the church when the rest went to the celebration of the sacrament."

So far this learned enquirer into, and writer of primitive Christianity, from who we may positively infer that no unbaptized person was by the ancients admitted to the Communion of the Lord's Supper.

Shewing that this Opinion that Unbaptized Persons may be Admitted to the Lord's Supper, is *Against the Practice of All Christians in All Ages* that have Owned Ordinances.

It is true that about the third century, from a fatal mistake of John 3:5, "Except a man be born of water and of the Spirit, he cannot enter into the Kingdom of God." Some began to bring in infant baptism, conceiving (as Cyprian and his disciples taught them) that no person small or great could be saved without it, and that it blotted out all sins committed before its administration. Hence Nazianzen exhorts against infant baptism unless in case of apparent danger of death. When this dismal error once took place, how many mischiefs did follow it, as

1. The subjects of baptism were changed from actual believers to ignorant babes, and the church altered in its primitive constitution, viz., from persons professing the faith, to a mixture of both converted and unconverted ones.

2. It being conceived that the old manner of administration by dipping, might be dangerous to young infants, and to the people that superstitiously delayed their baptism until their deathbed (because they believed it would take away all sin) therefore they contrived sprinkling to serve the turn for the infant, as well as those sick people, which were called Clinici, from the beds or hammocks they lay in; upon which Mr. Rogers writes thus: "He betrays the church to a disordered error, if he cleave not to the institution, to dip the infant in water, and this I so aver as thinking it (viz. DIPPING) exceeding material to the ordinance, and no slight thing, yea, which both antiquity, constantly and without exception of countries hot or cold, witnesses unto, and especially the constant word of the Holy Ghost, first and last approveth, as Causabon in Matt. 3:11 hath noted, etc., Treat. of Sacram. p. 77, "which misadministration came in time to be decreed by counsels, and imposed by fierce and severe anathema's, which is all the authority that can be produced (and which is indeed nothing at all to us that ought to have divine warrant for practical duties).

Now as the consequences of this error have been so fatal to the church of Christ, and as the prevalency of it was gradual (yet

Shewing that this Opinion that Unbaptized Persons may be Admitted to the Lord's Supper, is *Against the Practice of All Christians in All Ages* that have Owned Ordinances

so forcible was Truth that they kept the order, though they missed the subject), so it ought to be a very serious warning to us, to oppose all the beginnings of error, that is "to contend earnestly for the faith once delivered to the saints," because when error is once admitted, it comes with a fair and specious mask or vizard on, to disguise its deformity, till it spreads like a gangrene and infects the whole.

So this opinion comes disguised with the plausible allegation of charity and brotherly love, etc.

But was not the same pretense mainly made use of for the introducing infant baptism, viz., charity to the children's souls, whom they judged in a state of damnation without it, and certainly of the two, the introducers of Paedo-baptism are more excusable than the bringers-in of this opinion, because, although they missed the right subject of baptism, and attributed too much of it, yet they kept up a practice of that name in its due rank and order in the church, whereas these, on the other hand dispense with the total neglect of baptism, since baptism in infancy is by them held for no baptism for unanswerable reasons, as for instance. In baptism the Covenant struck between God and us implies, especially the consent of parties, but by infant baptism the infant is not bound, for he consented not. Again consent must be expressed, but the child wants the just ripeness and formation of organs inward and outward for such expressions, and so cannot will it, because he cannot understand it, nor can he express that which within him he hath not: Nor can he depute others to consent for him, nor is there any authority for such a deputation given by God, nor any instance in the sacred records that it was ever practiced. Nor can such as undertake it, perform what they promise for the child, viz., faith and repentance, being the two great graces of the gospel, and the sole gift of God. Besides Christ looks for a believer, which no infant can at present be said to be, the want of which, makes the baptism null, for if there be no bond, no Covenant, no obligation in it (as 'tis plain there is not, and they confess it) then there is no sealing, for a seal serves but

Shewing that this Opinion that Unbaptized Persons may be Admitted to the Lord's Supper, is *Against the Practice of All Christians in All Ages* that have Owned Ordinances.

to ratify and confirm a bond and covenant, and as there is no sealing, so there is no exhibition or conveyance of anything from Christ, for there are no pipes to receive it, that is, as an ordinance, there is no reason in the use of it, no faith, no sense, no receptive faculty proportionable to the ordinance in the manner of conveying it, etc. So that the conclusion is, that infant baptism is as much a nullity as the marrying or ordination of infants, and being really so by the grant of the favorers of this opinion: it will unavoidably follow that their admitting persons, upon pretense of that baptism to the Lord's Supper, is neither more nor less than an admission without baptism, and a plain declaration that they esteem this ordinance to be unnecessary and consequently a direct throwing it out of the church as was said before, so that Paedobaptism, is but a perverting or an abuse of the ordinance of baptism, but this opinion quite abolishes it, which is the necessary effect and consequence of their declaring it to be needless in order to admission into a church, etc.

But to return we can have no better instances of the practice of antiquity, than what we find recorded of the Cathecumeni, who were excluded not only from the Eucharist, but from the very sign thereof; and therefore after the words "holy things to saints," they went out, not because they were without faith, for there were two sorts, viz., hearers, and such as were competent or elect; the first were beginners which heard sermons, and had a desire to Christ; the other were such as desired baptism, and had given up their names for it, as Austin and others mention.

Now these were suppose to have faith, and waited only a fit time for the administration of baptism, during which time they were not at all admitted to the Lord's Supper, though judged believers, but as soon as baptized, they were admitted to the Lord's Supper on the same day also.

To *Illustrate this Point* Further We Will Give a Brief Abstract of Some Things Recorded in that Excellent History Compiled by the Divines of Madeburg.

Basil writes, that there were no others but Cathechumens baptized who were called together at Easter.

Such as were to be baptized in the churches of Asia were first for some time instructed in the doctrine of piety, and were called Catechumens: as we have before fore recited it from Basil. Let us receive (sayeth he) the grace of resurrection in the day of resurrection. For that reason the church with a loud voice calls together from afar, those she brings up, that such as were brought forth naught, may at length by the milk of sound doctrine being catechumens nourished by faith, be strengthened by the taste of more solid food and perfect institution. And there again, we must know (says he) that it is necessary, first to teach and instruct, and afterwards dignify (or vouchsafe to) him that is so rightly instructed, with the most excellent baptism.

Athanasius declares, the same thing of the Jews, that they cast themselves at the feet of the Bishop of that city (v. where they lived) and desired baptism, whom when he and his clergy beheld, he instructed them for many days in the Doctrine of Christian Piety and being thereby made catechumens after three days fast he baptized them.

This practice of catechising, and then baptizing, and afterwards receiving into church-fellowship was so universal among all the Christians of those times, as appears by these

To *Illustrate this Point* Further We Will Give a Brief Abstract of Some Things Recorded in that Excellent History Compiled by the Divines of Madeburg.

few instances, and many more cited from Athanasius, Nazianzen, Optatus, Milevitanus, Epiphanius, Hillarius, Ambrose, Jerome, Sozomen and others, that we find no opposition at all to it; all candidates for Christianity being that way only admitted; the necessity of it being reputed so great, that it became the very inlet of Paedo-baptism. So that the conclusion is undoubted that we have got above four hundred years of primitive antiquity, to witness our practice.

And in the Fifth Century Augustine gives the sense of that Age thus. "Let them (that is the Catechumens) passed through the Red Sea, that is, be baptized, and let them eat manna, that is the body and blood of the Lord."

And in the Seventh Century, Isidorus de Officiis makes three degrees. The first is, "Of the Cathechumens, who were such as were first come from gentilism, and had a mind to believe in Christ. The second of Competents, who desired baptism, when they were instructed in the Doctrine of Christ. And the third, of the baptized, who were then church-members."

Haymo says, in Century Nine (In cap. 1 ad Ephes. Catechumei sunt fideles quia credunt in verum Deum; sed quia nondum baptizati, non sunt Sancti.) "That the Catechumes are the faithful because they believe in the true God; but because they are not baptized, they are not holy."

But what needs any more of these quotations, when all that know anything of the practice of antiquity must confess, that this opinion we oppose, was never in the world for sixteen hundred years and more. For though an antichristian darkness overspread the greatest part of Christendom for a long time, and infant baptism almost crowded that true and Apostolical practice of Believer's Baptism out of the church; though Lodovicus Vives says, "That the custom of baptizing adult persons was yearly practiced in Rome itself, even in his time." Yet the very Papists all along (as they do at this time) retained this as the initiating ordinance; all their writings, canons, decrees, etc., cry up baptism, to be not only

To *Illustrate this Point* Further We Will Give a Brief Abstract of Some Things Recorded in that Excellent History Compiled by the Divines of Madeburg.

necessary to church-communion, but even to salvation.

Yea, all the Reformers, whether Lutherans, Calvinists or other foreigners, the Church of England, and all of the dissenting congregations that own ordinances (except a few persons of the baptized way and that lately, too) have owned, and do own, that baptism is an ordinance of Christ; yea, the very first, or initiating ordinance into church-fellowship, without which no man may be regularly admitted to the Supper.

So that this opinion is not only against us, but contradictory to the judgment and practice of all other Christians, ancient and modern. Baptism was of old, and not without reason, called the Gate of Sacraments, and is to keep that name and nature still, viz., to be the first and primitive ordinance. If the timing and order of instituted worship be anything, as it is of great moment, a great part of it lying in nothing else, but the right and orderly administration of ceremonies, and if the Scripture rule and example be anything (which is all we have to shew for any practice), then baptism is to be the first ordinance after believing.

If the testimony of ancient records and modern writers of all sorts, unanimously makes out that there has not been any other practice in fact among Christians all along, than what we here demonstrate, though that is not brought by itself to prove the same, it is certainly a very fair collateral inforcement and illustration: for there is no point of religion debated in the world, that has a more clear and universal concurrence of sixteen hundred years complete, than, that no persons were received to the communion of the Lord's Supper or church-fellowship, unless they were first baptized. Yea, such a value had antiquity for this ordinance, that such as were baptized by heretics, as the Arians and others, that used not the name of Christ, or (otherwise) defectively performed it, were judged by the most learned men of their times to be unbaptized, and therefore were baptized again by such as were orthodox, when they left their heresies, which is

To *Illustrate this Point* Further We Will Give a Brief Abstract of Some Things Recorded in that Excellent History Compiled by the Divines of Madeburg.

so well known that it needs no instances.

To conclude this chapter, we shall give a few instances of some modern writers besides what are given before, not so much deriving authority from them (though they deserve all due respect) but because of the solidity and force of their reasonings.

A very noted and learned author now living writes thus, "(1.) If we have neither precept nor example in Scripture since Christ ordained baptism, of any other way of admitting visible members, but only by baptism, than all that must be admitted visible members, must be ordinarily baptized: but since baptism was instituted (or established) we have no precept or example of admitting visible members any other way (but constant precept and example of admitting this way; John 4:1; Acts 2:38, 41; 8:12, 13, 16, 36, 38; 9:18; 10:47, 48; 16:15, 33; 18:8; 19:3, 4; Rom. 6:3, etc.): therefore all that must be admitted visible members, must be baptized.

I know not what in any shew of reason can be said to this by those that renounce not Scripture. For what man dare go in a way which hath neither precept nor example to warrant it, from a way that hath a full current of both? yet they that will admit members into the visible church without baptism, do so.

2. Either members must be baptized at their admission or else after they are stated in the church, or else never. But the two later are false: therefore it must be the former way, viz., at their admission.

(1.) That they should never be baptized, none will affirm but the seekers, and they that are above ordinances (that is, above obedience to God, and so gods.)

(2.) If they say they must be baptized after they are stated in the church (and that many years as they would have it) I answer (1.) shew any Scripture for that if you can. (2.) It is

To *Illustrate this Point* Further We Will Give a Brief Abstract of Some Things Recorded in that Excellent History Compiled by the Divines of Madeburg.

contrary to all Scripture example, Acts 2. The three thousand were presently baptized, and the jailer at the same hour of the night, and so of all the rest. And if you could shew any that did delay it, (since Christ's command, Matt. 28:20) it would appear to have been sinful, as through ignorance or negligence; so that then it must needs be done at their first admittance according to the constant course of Scripture.

3. It is evident also from the very nature and end of baptism, which is to be Christ's listing and engaging sign; and therefore must be applied when we enter His army.

4. If we are (Jews and Gentiles, etc.) baptized into one body, then we are not to delay it till we are stated in the body; but we are all baptized into one body, (1 Cor. 12:13), therefore, etc. For if it be the use of baptism to engraft and enter us into the body or church (and into Christ, as Rom. 6:3), than sure it must be used as our engrafting and entrance. Shall a soldier be listed two or three years after he hath been in the army, or at the first entrance, whether?

5. If all church members are Christ's disciples, and all disciples must be baptized (at their admission) then all church-members must be baptized at their admission: but all church-members are disciples, and all disciples must be baptized at their admission, therefore all church-members must be baptized at their admission.

(1.) That disciples must be baptized at their admission is plain (Matt. 28:19, 20). Disciple all nations baptizing them, and by constant example. (2.) That all church-members are disciples I prove thus, (1) If it be the church which is Christ's school, than all members of the church are His scholars or disciples, or members of His school: but it is only the church which is called Christ's school; therefore all church-members are school-members, or disciples, (2) And thus if all church members are Christians, and all Christians are Christ's disciples, than all church members are Christ's Disciples: but all church-members are Christians, and all

To *Illustrate this Point* Further We Will Give a Brief Abstract of Some Things Recorded in that Excellent History Compiled by the Divines of Madeburg.

Christians are Christ's disciples: therefore all church-members are Christ's disciples, (1) That all church-members (true ones) are Christians, that is retainers to Christ, or such as belong to Christ (as his own phrase is) is beyond doubt, (2) That all Christians are disciples I proved before, it being the plain words of the Holy Ghost (Acts 11:26). The disciples were called Christians first at Antioch; so that all church-members being disciples, they must regularly be baptized at their admission, according to the course of Scripture, and my text (Matt. 28:19,20).

6. Another argument may be plainly fetched from Ephesians 5:26. That he might sanctify it, and cleanse it (His church) by the washing of water through the Word; If the whole church must be sanctified by the washing of water than all particular members of the church must be so sanctified; therefore the individual members."

He further writes thus, from Matthew 28:19. Go and disciple me all nations baptizing them, etc. "What Christ hath conjoined, man must not separate: But Christ hath conjoined discipling and baptizing, as a standing course to the end of the world (as the next verse speaks); therefore we must not separate them. Though the word [forever] do sometimes signify a limited time in the Old Testament, viz., till the New World under Christ; yet in the Gospel [till the end of the world] can have no other than the proper signification without plain impudent violence.

2. Argument 2 from 1 Cor. 12:13. By one Spirit we are all baptized into one body. If baptism be God's appointed ordinary way of engrafting all into the body of Christ, then it is a standing ordinance, as being of a standing use: but baptism is so, therefore, etc. the antecedent will appear plain in the text, if you consider first, that it is real baptism that is here mentioned; the Spirit being spoken of as a concurrent cause; secondly, that it was all that were thus baptized into the body.

To *Illustrate this Point* Further We Will Give a Brief Abstract of Some Things Recorded in that Excellent History Compiled by the Divines of Madeburg.

3. From Rom. 6:3. If the use of baptism be to baptize men into Jesus Christ, and into His death, then it is a standing ordinance to the church, as being of a standing use: but the former is in the text, therefore, etc.,

4. From Acts 2:38 and 22:16, If baptism be instituted for the remission of sin or the washing away of sin, (whether by signifying sealing or exhibiting) then it is a standing ordinance to the church; (as being to a standing use and end, one age of the church having no less need of it than another.) But the antecedent is in the text; therefore, etc.

5. If the end of baptism be our burial and resurrection with Christ (Col. 2:12); the churches salvation (1 Pet. 3:21); if a foundation principle (Heb. 6:2); The ordinary way of initiator putting on Christ (Gal. 3:27); then it is of continual use, and so a standing ordinance: but it is so, as the texts cited expressly say; therefore, etc.

6. If Christ himself has instituted the ordinance of baptism in the Word, and not again repealed it; then it is a standing ordinance to the church; (and no man must dare to repeal His laws) but Christ hath instituted; and let any man shew where he hath repealed it that can; and 'til then it must acknowledged to be still in force."

The learned and reverend Dr. Ames, in his <u>Marrow of Divinity,</u> page 181, says, "Baptism is the sacrament of initiation or regeneration, representing and confirming our very engrafting into Christ, Rom. 6:3, 5; 1 Cor. 12:13;" and p. 182, "Baptism is but once to be administered, because there is but one beginning of spiritual life by regeneration, as there is but one beginning of natural life by generation."

Paul Bayne, that holy learned man, on Col. 2:11, p. 280, says, "God doth unite us with Christ even by our baptism, that is," sayeth he, "the believer baptized, is by baptism manifested so before the church."

Elton on the same place, p. 291, "Baptism is the sacrament

To *Illustrate this Point* Further We Will Give a Brief Abstract of Some Things Recorded in that Excellent History Compiled by the Divines of Madeburg.

of incision or engrafting into Christ, sealing up our setting into Christ, which is only once, never after to be done again; for if it did not, then we should have another engrafting into Christ, and afterward nourished in him, therefore we often receive the ordinance of the Lord's Supper."

Dr. Owen in his Discourse of the Spirit, p. 50, where he, proving the Divine Nature and personality of the Holy Spirit, thus writes, viz.,

Section 11, "All things necessary to this purpose are comprised in the solemn form of our initiation into Covenant with God, Matt. 28:19, our Lord Jesus Christ commands his apostles to disciple all nations, baptizing them in the name of the Father, and the Son, and the Holy Ghost: this is the foundation we lay of all our obedience and profession, which are to be regulated by this initial engagement."

Section 14, p. 51, tells us, "We are sacredly initiated or consecrated, or dedicated unto the service and worship of the Father, Son and Holy Ghost, this we took upon us in our baptism, herein lies the foundation of our faith and profession with that engagement of ourselves unto God, which constitutes our Christianity. This is the pledge of our entering into Covenant with God, and our giving up ourselves unto him in the solemn bond of our religion."

Mr. Strong in his Discourse of the Covenants, p. 226, says, "Baptism is a sacrament of initiation and the ordinance of visible admission into the church; and that must not be done promiscuously, and without discrimination; for as it is a sin to keep out those whose right it is, so it's a sin also to admit them that have no right, because thereby the ordinances of Christ are abused and misplaced, where he never intended them, and for whom he never instituted them."

And p. 306, "We are said to be baptized into the name of them all (viz., Father, Son and Spirit) Matt. 28:20, Baptizing them in the name of the Father, and of the Son,

To *Illustrate this Point* Further We Will Give a Brief Abstract of Some Things Recorded in that Excellent History Compiled by the Divines of Madeburg.

and of the Holy Ghost: Now what is it to be baptized into the name of the Father: it's conceived to be taken from the manner of marriage, wherein the wife doth transpire in nomen, in familiam, etc., into the name and family of the husband: or of servants who had their masters name called upon them; and therefore no man might be baptized in the name of a creature, it is that which Paul detests, that he should baptize in his own name; and therefore the meaning is, to be baptized in fidem, in cultum, into the faith and worship of God, and so you are unto them all, and give up your names unto them all; and therefore unto each person we owe both faith and worship distinctly, all manner of duty and obedience, because we are distinctly baptized into the faith of them all, etc."

Dr. Manton, in his excellent sermons on Psalms 119:8, p. 45, In the prosecution of his doctrine, viz., "That it is a great advantage to come to a resolution in a course of godliness, faith, that it is a course God will bless, He hath appointed ordinances to this end and purpose that we might come to this resolution. The promise is first implicitly made in baptism, therefore it is called, 1 Pet. 3:21, the answer of a good conscience towards God. How so? Why the Covenant binds mutually on God's part and on ours; and so do the seals which belong to the covenant. It doth not only seal pardon and sanctification on God's part, but there is a promise and answer on our part: an answer to what? To the demands of the covenant. In the Covenant of Grace, God sayeth I will be your God (baptism seals that) and we promise to be His people. Now our answer to this demand of God, and to this interrogatory he puts to us in the Covenant, it is sealed by us in baptism; and it is renewed in the Lord's Supper, etc."

Mr. Burroughs, on Hosea 8:12, gives us this observation, "That whatever is urged to us or practiced by us in matter of worship must have warrant out of the written Word of God (it was sin) and why? Because I have written to them (sayeth He) the great things of my law, and they counted it a strange thing though that which they did had a great deal of

To *Illustrate this Point* Further We Will Give a Brief Abstract of Some Things Recorded in that Excellent History Compiled by the Divines of Madeburg.

seeming devotion in it, yet it was otherwise than that which was written in the Law.

This question should be put to any that tender to us any way of worship or doctrine of religion under any specious shew whatsoever, where is it written? Isaiah 8:20, If they speak not according to the word, 'tis because they have no light in them. Oh, they seem to be very judicious and wise, but if they speak not according to the word, it's because there is no light in them, to the written law and testimony, that must be the standard at which all doctrine and ways of worship must be tried, many may put fair colors upon the way, that it is for common peace, and a great deal of good may be done by it, and the like. But is it written? Did I ever command it? sayeth God. Policy may say 'tis fit; reason may say 'tis comely; and experience may say 'tis useful: but what doth the written Word say it should be? Nay it is not enough to say that we cannot say 'tis forbidden; but where is it written in matters of worship? This is a certain rule, sayeth Tertullian, If it be said 'tis lawful, because the Scripture doth not forbid it, it may equally be retorted; it is therefore not lawful, because the Scripture doth not command it."

And further, that reverend author, p. 86, notes from Ex. 39 at least ten times in that chapter, "They did according to what the Lord commanded Moses, and in verse 43, Moses blessed the people. The people are blessed when in the matters of worship they keep unto what is commanded."

This was the judgment of that famous servant of God, although no man in his time (as those that knew him in his life can testify) was of a more tender and bearing spirit to heal differences than he; yet how zealous and careful was he to advise and inculcate into the minds of Christians, that they should exactly keep to the written word in matters of God's instituted worship.

By what is said (Christian Reader), it evidently appears what a value all Christians in all ages, yea, at this day, have had for this great ordinance of baptism and how universally

To *Illustrate this Point* Further We Will Give a Brief Abstract of Some Things Recorded in that Excellent History Compiled by the Divines of Madeburg.

concurrent their testimonies are, that it is not only the sacrament of initiation, but also to be continued in the church unto the end of the world. And because it would swell this small piece beyond its intended bulk to use so great a cloud of witnesses, we shall add a few general and comprehending testimonies.

1. In the Articles of Religion published by His Majesty's special command 1642, baptism is thus defined, "Baptism is not only a sign of a profession, and mark of difference, whereby Christian men are discerned from others that be not christened: but it is also a sign of regeneration or new birth, whereby as by an instrument, they that receive baptism rightly are grafted into the church, the promises of the forgiveness of sin; and of our adoption to be the Sons of God by the Holy Ghost, and visibly signed and sealed: faith is confirmed, and grace increased by virtue of prayer unto God, etc." This is the judgment of the Church of England.

"The Assembly of Divines in their Confession of Faith printed 1658, p. 94, define baptism a sacrament of the New Testament ordained by Jesus Christ (Matt. 28:19) not only for the solemn admission of the party baptized into the visible church (1 Cor. 12:13), but also to be unto him a sign and seal of the Covenant of Grace (Col. 2:12), of his engrafting into Christ (Gal. 3:17); of regeneration (Titus 3:5); of remission of sins (Mark 1:4); and of his giving up unto God through Jesus Christ, to walk in newness of life (Rom. 6:3,4); which sacrament is by Christ's own appointment to continue in His church, until the end of the world, Matt. 28:19,20. This is the judgment of the Presbyterians: suitable to which they express themselves in their Larger Catechism, p. 128, and in the Shorter Catechism, p. 157.

The Congregational (commonly called Independent) churches, in their Confession of Faith at the Savoy, where were many of their elders, Oct., 1658, printed 1659, thus say of baptism, "Baptism is a sacrament of the New Testament ordained by Jesus Christ to be unto the party baptized a sign and

To *Illustrate this Point* Further We Will Give a Brief Abstract of Some Things Recorded in that Excellent History Compiled by the Divines of Madeburg.

seal of the Covenant of Grace, of his engrafting into Christ, of regeneration, of remission of sins, and of his giving up unto God through Jesus Christ to walk in newness of life; which ordinance is by Christ's own appointment to be continued in His church until the end of the world."

The churches of Christ commonly (though unjustly) called Anabaptists, in their Confession of Faith (Fourth Impression printed 1652), define baptism "an ordinance of the New Testament given by Christ to be dispensed upon persons professing faith, or that are made disciples; who upon profession of faith, and desiring of it, ought to be baptized, and after to partake of the Lord's Supper."

OBJECTION, If it should be objected, To what purpose serve all these quotations since the parties you dispute against do believe and hold, that baptism is an ordinance of Christ and keep up the practice of it.

ANSWER, 1. Although they hold and practice it themselves, yet in the effect and consequence of this their opinion, they deny it: for whilst they allege, that it is not requisite to church communion, it must of necessity be understood, that they judge it not a requisite duty for a Christian; and consequently, 'tis needless and therefore may be laid aside without danger, which is in effect a total casting of it away: which is not only contradictory to Scripture, but disagreeable to all other Christians in the world, as hath been fully made out.

2. If they hold baptism to be a Christian duty, I would ask, Whether it be the duty of all Christians, or only some? If of all, how can it be dispensed with in any? If only of some, viz., such as are convinced of it; it will equally follow, by the same reason, that no ordinance at all, is a duty to a person that doubts either the thing itself, or the manner or circumstances of its practice. And if it be not duty, no man may be blamed for the nonperformance of it, but indeed would sin in doing it, and so by consequence, no ordinance is binding to all, because there is not one of them, but is in some respect or other

To *Illustrate this Point* Further We Will Give a Brief Abstract of Some Things Recorded in that Excellent History Compiled by the Divines of Madeburg.

cavilled at, or at least not rightly understood by some persons that yet would be esteemed godly: so that this opinion opens a gap, not only for exclusion of baptism, but of any ordinance whatsoever, under the pretense of a large charity to a doubting person, that is really holy, or seems so to be. But the Lord never left His ordinances upon such terms; for they are not to be dispensed with upon any pretense whatsoever without his own special warrant.

Suitable to what we here write, Henry Lawrence Esq., a very judicious and learned writer expressed himself, in his Book of Baptism, p. 368, ch. 17, thus, that there is an order in the worship of the New Testament: (says he) "No man will deny that hath learned with Paul, to join beholding the order and faith of saints, Col. 2:5. And now "will acknowledge this more than they who deny themselves of some very considerable ordinances for want of coming to them in the right order, as the Lord's Supper for want of church fellowship: everything is seasonable and beautiful in its time, out of which it is disorderly and evil, to find the order and time of baptism will I conceive be the easiest thing in all this inquiry, whether you consider Scripture rule, Scripture example, or example of the primitive church, or indeed of all that ever was, or the reason of things; for Scripture rule you have Matt. 28:19, Make disciples and baptize; Mark 16:16, He that believeth and is baptized shall be saved. You see here the rank of baptism, immediately after teaching, after believing, it holds the first place of ordinances properly Christian, you may see it again in the rule of Peter's preaching, Acts 2:38.

For the primitive times we can have no better instances, than what we have of the catechuminy, who were excluded not only from the Eucharist, but from the very sight thereof, etc.

And of this the fathers give a reason, viz., in all respects the order of the mystery is kept, that first by remission of sins, a medicine be prepared for their wounds, and then the nourishment of the heavenly table be added ambrose, etc.

To *Illustrate this Point* Further We Will Give a Brief Abstract of Some Things Recorded in that Excellent History Compiled by the Divines of Madeburg.

If you pass from precept and example of all times to reason, there you will find that whatever makes for the not repeating of baptism in the ordinary use of it, makes also for this as fully, or more, that it should be the first.

For first, if it be not to be repeated, because this is the seal of initiation, regeneration, and incorporation, then by the same reason this must be first as initiation, admission, incorporation, and regeneration, are the first internal acts in us, and upon us, by which we are made Christians.

Secondly, if the significations, and use of baptism be forever and of constant and perpetual use, then this ordinance is to lie as the bottom stone in the Building of ordinances, which is to have a durable and constant influence into the whole edifice.

Thirdly, if this be not to be repeated, because neither in precept nor example you find it so, and never otherwise, or if the ends of baptism on our part, be that there shall be a formal external contract passed with God, by which we are visibly handfasted in this mystical marriage. Or, 2. To distinguish ourselves by this badge and character of our profession from the evil world, which we renounce with all its works, then certainly this piece is to be first administered before we go further, and the sacrament of our spiritual life and birth is to be given before that of our nourishment: In a word baptism hath been called of old, and not without reason, sacramentorum janua, and is for all these considerations, which are as many as concur to any one thing to keep that name and nature still, which is to be the first and primitive sacrament, in which a converted person, man or woman, is to communicate. Now then if the timing and order of instituted worship be anything, as it is of great moment, a great part of it lying in nothing else but the right and orderly administration of ceremonies; and if the Scripture rule and example be anything, which is all we have to shew for any practice; then baptism is to be the first sacrament after believing: besides the reason of the thing, that which

To *Illustrate this Point* Further We Will Give a Brief Abstract of Some Things Recorded in that Excellent History Compiled by the Divines of Madeburg.

makes it unlawful to baptize before teaching is because the Scripture hath ranked it otherwise, that says teach and baptize, not baptize and teach, as the Papists and others do, the same reason will hold for the giving it its preference in time to any other ordinance, because it's ranked immediately after teaching, and before any other thing." Thus far you have the opinion and reason of that learned gentleman.

Chapter Five

Wherein the *Objections Against this Position* viz., that None May be Regularly Admitted to the Lord's Supper, that are not First Baptized, *are Answered.*

OBJECTION 1. There is no rule, or express warrant of Scripture to exclude persons fearing God, from receiving the Lord's Supper, who by virtue of their faith have a right to it.

Answer. This objection supposes things very dangerous, as, 1. That holiness without baptism invests a right to other church ordinances, which is not to be supposed, for Christ the Lamb of God was Holy in the highest degree, and in Him was found no sin, yet He was baptized before He entered upon His public ministry (Matt. 3:15, 16), which is a most illustrious example, and the pattern which the saints followed; for in a word, the great apostle Paul and all those primitive saints recorded by the Spirit to be believers, and therefore holy; were nevertheless baptized, which might have been forborn but that it was an indispensable duty: and whatsoever reason may be given, why holiness without baptism may serve, the like may be produced, why holiness without any other ordinance may be sufficient for a believer? And unless it be less necessary now for believers to perform gospel duties, then for evangelical saints; or unless it can be made out, that baptism was only appointed for that age (as holy an age as

Wherein the *Objections Against this Position* viz., that None May be Regularly Admitted to the Lord's Supper, that are not First Baptized, *are Answered.*

ever was), the obligation of practicing that duty still lies upon all Christians, which is a warrant and rule for the exclusion of such as will not submit to it.

2. It supposes, that whatsoever is not forbidden in Scripture is lawful; and so the receiving of believers that are not baptized to the Supper, being not prohibited, is therefore lawful.

Now that this is a pernicious way of argument, has been largely demonstrated about the beginning, as tending to bring all human inventions into God's worship, to which we refer: yet doubtless, it will be granted by all that the only warrant we have (as has been frequently said), for the practice of gospel duties, must be the express warrant, or Word of God, according to which we must walk: and I very well remember, that the old Nonconformists who faithfully followed the Lord according to the light they had received, rather than they would kneel at the sacrament, thought it their duty to forbear the practice of that great ordinance, giving this as their reason: To leave (say they) the practice of Christ and His apostles in the manner of receiving the sacrament, and to follow the practice of men, in a posture invented by men is not safe: but to kneel at the sacrament is so, etc., therefore not safe.

And if the servants of God in those times were so cautious of doing anything that might be an addition to the worship of God although but in a circumstance: how much ought Christians now when the matter is about the very order of the practice of ordinances themselves; for here in the case in hand, is a most evident leaving the practice of Christ and His apostles, and following the inventions of men.

2. The Commission given by Christ, Matt. 28:19, Go teach all nations baptizing them, etc. hath been an argument of great weight in the minds of all that oppose infant baptism, the order of the words shewing who are to be baptized, viz., such as are taught; first teach, then baptize: and if it be an argument, that proves believers baptism only, it must have its

Wherein the *Objections Against this Position* viz., that None May be Regularly Admitted to the Lord's Supper, that are not First Baptized, *are Answered.*

consideration, that baptism must go before the practice of other ordinances, as preaching goes before baptism.

We find Acts 1:3 that Jesus Christ was forty days with His disciples, speaking of the things pertaining to the Kingdom of God; and doubtless He was not wanting in giving them direction concerning the order of His worship. For as the Commission (Matt. 28:19) was given after His resurrection, we may see His apostles (as appears by their constant administration suitable thereto) did practice no other way, as Acts 2:41, 42 and several other places fully produced before. Which practice in order to the receiving or enjoying of ordinances, I take to be a constant and a standing direction for all churches, in all times, unless any can shew a variation from it, by any of the primitive churches afterwards, which cannot be done; I would fain know of him that preaches the gospel to men, what doctrine he is to preach to them? Is it any other than to believe and be baptized; if no other (as I judge all will grant), than if in case the party believing should question whether water baptism be the ordinance of Jesus Christ, or if he believes it, is not yet satisfied it is his duty to be baptized, but desires he may break bread with the church, can this without a manifest breach of the rule be admitted.

The apostle tells us, Gal. 3:27, That as many of you as have been baptized into Christ, have put on Christ, that is, they have put on (The Verb signifies to put on as a garment) Christ as a garment, and by baptism have put on the visible profession of Christ, plainly holding out, that none have put on the visible profession of Christ until they be baptized; the outward sign, answering to the inward grace, so Rom. 6:3, Know ye not that we who were baptized into Jesus Christ were baptized into His death: which baptism is a pledge of. Can it therefore be judged upon any reasonable pretence that any man should be admitted to walk in the practice of the ordinances of Christ, before he hath put on Christ in the visible profession of His name by baptism.

Wherein the *Objections Against this Position* viz., that None May be Regularly Admitted to the Lord's Supper, that are not First Baptized, *are Answered.*

From the whole of which we infer, in answer to the objection that our practice suitable to these precepts and examples, are a sufficient rule and warrant for our not admitting them to the Lord's Supper, and to call for Scripture precepts or examples for refusing them, is very absurd; for we may as well call for the like to warrant our separation from the Church of Rome by name, which can be produced no more than this, yet it does not follow, that communion with that church, as now it is, is lawful. Scripture examples are a matter of fact; and therefore, there having been no such corrupt practice crept into the world when the Scripture was written, therefore there was no occasion for any baptized person to disclaim communion with the unbaptized; there being no such cause of which to make an example.

OBJECTION 2. But we admit none to the supper of the Lord, but those that think they are baptized already, and judge what they received in their infancy sufficient.

ANSWER. It is certain that they who believe that the only subjects of baptism are actual believers, viz., such who upon a profession of faith received that ordinance, and esteemed no other baptism valid, cannot judge the baptism received in infancy to be Christ's baptism, they knowing that the proper subject appointed by Christ, viz., a believer (which is the main part of the essence of the ordinance) is wanting, and certainly the ground of churches proceedings, in admitting persons to the Supper cannot be built upon the imagination of the party desiring communion, but upon the knowledge the church hath of it, and its being tried by the rule which they are to walk by. For,

Suppose a person desires to sit down as a member of the church, as thinking he hath a true faith, and a right to the privilege in the church, when yet he can give no satisfactory demonstration of either; will any think the church ought to receive him because he hath that good persuasion of himself, when they themselves are satisfied that what he declares is insufficient by the rule, to make out his right? Or will any

Wherein the *Objections Against this Position* viz., that None May be Regularly Admitted to the Lord's Supper, that are not First Baptized, *are Answered.*

judgment of charity warrant such a proceeding? Certainly no; and yet the reason is the same for the latter, as for the former. Besides the consequence to the party that should be so admitted to the Supper upon his conceit that he is baptized is very dangerous, and must needs build him up in the conceit that he hath that which indeed he hath not. God of old gave this charge, that a stumbling-block must not be put in the way of the blind, and surely a greater stumbling-block cannot be put in such men's way to hinder their inquiry after the true baptism of Christ than to admit of that supposition, which the church knoweth is not true. For having now the enjoyment of all the privileges of the House of God, they hereby are forever careless of making any further inquiry: and I heartily wish that this maybe seriously considered by those that exercise this groundless charity.

Again, suppose the child of a baptized person of sufficient age, that was brought up in a godly manner, is converted and become a believer, yet was never baptized at all, should propose for communion with the church, would they admit him without baptism, if he desires communion so (not being satisfied, that it is a necessary duty)? If they would, then it is evident, that they quite exclude baptism out of the rank of ordinances; if they do not admit him, then they place a sufficiency in infant baptism, because they grant a privilege to him that had it, and deny the same to him that had it not, (whom we do suppose to be as much a believer, and as holy as the other), which is expressly against their own principle, viz., to esteem infant baptism as no baptism; and therefore if they hold to it, should place him that was so in infancy baptized, and him that was never baptized, in the same rank, with respect to the privilege of church communion.

OBJECTION 3. It is said, Rom. 14:1, Him that is weak in the faith, receive you, and it being but the weakness of such persons to judge their own baptism lawful, yet being such as have faith, this Scripture sufficiently warrants us to receive them.

Wherein the *Objections Against this Position* viz., that None May be Regularly Admitted to the Lord's Supper, that are not First Baptized, *are Answered.*

ANSWER. For the right understanding of this text, two things ought to be considered, which if well weighed may give a clear answer to this Scripture objection.

1. What weakness this is, which the Apostle here intends.

2. What is to be understood by receiving such.

1. The weakness spoken of in the text, hath relation only to those mistakes that did attend some of them touching a liberty of eating, or not eating meats, or the keeping or not keeping of days which were things in themselves of an indifferent nature, the doing or not doing of which, was not sin, as the apostle in that chapter plainly shews; and hath no relation to the order of worship prescribed by Christ, much less to the practice or not practice of ordinances, for then the meaning of the Apostle should be, if they did practice, or not practice, it was all one, there was no sin in the matter.

2. The receiving here cannot be meant to receive into the church as members, because the Apostle writes this epistle to the church and these weak members as a part of that church; but the receiving here intended is into the affections of each other; that the differences that were amongst them should not hinder the Law of Love, which they, and every Christian ought to cherish and exercise towards each other, let their differences be of what nature they will: that this must be the sense of the Apostle, the clear scope of the whole chapter makes evident. But to bring this text to prove a lawfulness of receiving any that are Christians although never so ignorant of the ordinances, and instituted worship of Christ, and the order prescribed by Him is to wring blood out of it, and not that precious truth that is manifested by it.

OBJECTION 4. Whereas some infer from 1 Cor. 12:13. By one Spirit we are all baptized into one body, whether Jews or Gentiles, bond or free, and have been all made to drink into one spirit, etc. That baptism is the enchurching

Wherein the *Objections Against this Position* viz., that None May be Regularly Admitted to the Lord's Supper, that are not First Baptized, *are Answered.*

ordinance, the conclusion is impertinent, for not water baptism, but the baptism of the Spirit is there meant.

ANSWER. That baptism was of so constant and universal use to the enchurching of all sorts ranks and degrees, is fairly deduced from this text, however excepted against and that none were enchurched without it, unless any man can find or name some persons that were neither Jew nor Gentiles, bond nor free, which denotes plainly, that all sorts were received by baptism: the Jews though before circumcised, yet were baptized; the Gentiles, sometimes a people afar off were upon their believing by baptism received. If free, as masters, yet not admitted without it; if bond, as servants, yet by this ordinance they were made equally of the same church privilege by baptism, Gal. 3:27, 28.

And that water baptism is here meant is the judgment of the most learned expositors: and the next words do make it appear, We have been all made to drink into one Spirit. By being baptized into one body and made to drink into one spirit. The Apostle shews the Communion which believers have with the Holy Spirit in the two ordinances, baptism and the Lord's Supper. For what else can be intended by drinking into one spirit, but the saint's communion in the spirit, in, and by the Supper [drinking] by a synecdoche being put both for eating and drinking; and if so, why must we not as well understand the first ordinance in its proper sense for water baptism in the former part, as the later ordinance, the Supper in the first part of the text.

2. If the baptism of the Spirit had been meant, then the being baptized into one body, and drinking into one spirit, must be one and the same thing, but surely baptizing and drinking are no more the same, than the body and the spirit are the same, into which they are said respectively to be baptized, and to drink. But it is clear the Apostle hereby intends to mind those Corinthians, how that by means of the same spirit working upon all their hearts, they became members of the same body by baptism, and that being of the

Wherein the *Objections Against this Position* viz., that None May be Regularly Admitted to the Lord's Supper, that are not First Baptized, *are Answered.*

body, they came to have communion in spirit, or with the spirit in the Supper.

It cannot be the baptism of the Spirit, because the spirit is here set forth by the apostle, as the agent or working cause, and baptism as the effect; and it is ridiculous to make both cause and effect the same thing. It is true that Scripture speaks elsewhere of a being baptized with the Spirit, but when it doth so, it still declares either Jesus Christ, or God the Father as the Agent of baptizing with the Spirit, but never as making the Spirit both the subject matter wherewith, and the agent whereby, men are baptized in the same baptism, see Matt. 3:11; Mark 1:8; Luke 3:16; and 24:49; Acts 11:4,5,16.

We find in Scripture that when God chargeth men for sin, He tells them, they did that which He commanded not, neither did it enter in His heart. Now that this was the order of administration with respect to these ordinances, viz., 1. To teach, then baptize, and then admit to church-communion, is elsewhere fully evidenced from precept and example, Matt. 28:19; Acts 2:41, etc. And if that be the stated method of God, and the universal practice of the primitive Christians, we may rationally infer that the contrary practice is a deviation from the Divine Rule, and a thing which God commanded not.

The Apostle according to the Rule of Christ, first at Jerusalem, to put this commission in execution, Luke 24:47. And did act according to it, and certainly their punctual conformity to it, ought to be taken by us as the interpretation of this grand precept, and their example a sufficient pattern for succeeding Christians; unless we will suppose them to depart from it as soon as they began to act in pursuance of it, which supposition includes a very strange uncharitableness, and a very unbecoming opinion of these Holy men. For nothing can be more plain than that addition to the church (or church fellowship) followed after baptism, and did not go before it: and why men now find a greater good in their own way than in His, is not to be easily

Wherein the *Objections Against this Position* viz., that None May be Regularly Admitted to the Lord's Supper, that are not First Baptized, *are Answered.*

resolved. Baptism in those days did certainly precede church enjoyments, for it was esteemed (as it still ought to be) a means of implanting men into Christ, or the body of Christ the church, Gal. 3:27; Rom. 6:3. Now let it be considered what a planting together imports; it must be certainly the first putting of Christians together, in order to their growing together in Christ, and yet all this was done by baptism: and may we not suppose trees to grow together before they are planted together, as this spiritual plantation of Christ, viz., the Church, or Society of Christians, who were, and should still be planted together by baptism, not into this or that particular church; but into that one church of Christ, which is distributed into several parts and particular societies. Hence baptism is called one of the principles or beginning doctrines of Christ, and part of the foundation, Heb. 6:1,2. Now there is no house can stand without its principle, or can be erected without a foundation. See 1 Cor. 12:13. Where we have an account of all being baptized into one body, whether Jews or Gentiles, bond or free, which comprehended all ranks and degrees of Christians, as is elsewhere demonstrated.

OBJECTION 5. The phrase, Rom. 6:3 and Gal. 3:27 [As many] of you as have been baptized into Christ, etc., implies that all that were in those churches of Rome and Galatia were not baptized.

ANSWER. If we consult the Scripture with the coherence, it will appear how weak this objection is.

1. For that Rom. 6:3. Let it be considered to whom the Apostle writes: Is it not to the whole church, and every individual of them? In verse 1,2. When he says, "What shall we say then? Shall we continue in sin, that grace may abound? God forbid. How shall we that are dead to sin live any longer therein?" If these words in the first and second verse respect the whole church, as they must be supposed to do, unless we will conclude that the Apostle did grant a liberty to some of the church to continue in sin, and live therein, then these words, "Know ye not that as many of us as were baptized into Jesus

Wherein the *Objections Against this Position* viz., that None May be Regularly Admitted to the Lord's Supper, that are not First Baptized, *are Answered.*

Christ, etc.," are interrogatively propounded not only to the same persons, unto whom the former words relate, but also as an argument or reason why none of them should live any longer in sin, which is the thing from which he was dissuading not only some of them, but even all of them in the foregoing verses, and which he improves in an argumentative way throughout the greatest part of the chapter, and it would not befit the reason of any ordinary man, much less of a great apostle to make choice a reason or motive to enforce his exhortation or persuasion, which is of less extent in the tendency and concernment of it, than are the persons whom he doth exhort or dehort. Which yet is a piece of weakness, of which we must suppose this Apostle to be guilty, unless you do conclude that all those of the church of Rome were dissuaded from continuing any longer in sin upon this ground, because they had been all baptized into the death of Christ, viz., a conformity to His death, as well as a belief of it. To conclude, if the whole church had not been under the motive, the whole church could not be pressed by it as here you see they are.

As for the other text, Gal. 3:26, the apostle had assured them, viz., them to whom he now writes, To be all the children of God by faith in Christ Jesus, that is they were looked upon as children of God by their confessing and owning of Jesus Christ, of which he gives this account, verse 27. Because they had put on Christ in baptism, You are all the children of God by faith in Christ Jesus, for, or because, as many of you, as have been baptized into Christ, have put on Christ: as if he should say, if the owning and professing Christ does denominate men to be the children of God, now under the gospel, as indeed it does, then ye are all the children of God, because by being baptized into Christ, ye have all of you put Him on, that is, so to appear with Him, wherever ye become, as you do appear with the clothes you wear. But now most certain it is, they could not all of them have been denominated the children of God by faith in Christ, upon account of their being baptized into Christ (which yet

Wherein the *Objections Against this Position* viz., that None May be Regularly Admitted to the Lord's Supper, that are not First Baptized, *are Answered.*

we see they are) unless they had been all of them baptized into Christ indeed.

Besides in what hath been said already it does not appear that any in the apostle's days were enchurched without baptism. And for any to assert that some, not all, were baptized, is to affirm what is void of Scripture, reason, and common sense. As for any countenance in Scripture, there is none. And it has as little in reason: for if it should be true, it will follow that this great ordinance was a duty to some only, and not to all, and the reason why it should be so, will be very difficult to assign, was it because it was commanded to some only, and not others? If so, let them be instanced by some kind of record, who were obliged to the practice, and who not: was it because some only had need of it, and others not? or because those glorious mysteries represented by it, were useless to some, and not to all? Or what other reason was it? If none can be assigned, then we may safely conclude that all church-members were then baptized; and ought to be so still.

It is confessed that sometimes the phrase [as many] has not the same latitude of significations as the phrase [all men] which includes every individual, the term [as many] being restrained to matter going before being then partitive: but here it has relation to the whole scope of the text, and must therefore intend all, or all of that church to whom he wrote, to confirm which interpretation we find other texts [as many] must of necessity be so understood as 1 Tim. 6:1 "Let as many servants as are under the yoke, count their own masters worthy of all honor:" doth he thereby suppose or may it be implied that there were some servants who were not under the yoke, or that there were some servants who were not to count their masters worthy of all honor? But which must be supposed notwithstanding, if this form or manner of speaking (as many as) be always to be understood to intend the dividing of the entire number of persons spoken unto; which yet to suppose must needs be very absurd.

Wherein the *Objections Against this Position* viz., that None May be Regularly Admitted to the Lord's Supper, that are not First Baptized, *are Answered.*

OBJECTION. And if it be said, that this exhortation, let as many servants as etc. doth intentionally respect so many believing servants as were under the yoke; and that therefore in respect of other believers it is partitive.

ANSWER. If that be granted there will be more gained then otherwise: for then it may well be said, that those texts, Rom. 6:3; Gal. 3:27. Intentionally, only respected those at Rome and Galatia, who did believe, and were baptized; and therefore is partitive in respect of others, the inhabitants of those places, dividing those of the churches, from others dwelling in the same places, who were not of those churches.

OBJECTION 6. If it be objected from Acts 9:26 that we find not there, when Paul was presented to the church at Jerusalem, and assayed to join himself to the disciples, that the church made any inquiry whether he was baptized or no, in order to his reception amongst them; or that Barnabus in giving satisfaction to the Apostles and the church concerning his meetness to be admitted into communion with them, so much as mentions his being baptized, but only declareth unto them, how he had seen the Lord in the way, and that He had spoken to him, and how he had preached boldly at Damascus in the name of Jesus.

ANSWER. There is no good reason can be given, or to suppose that Paul was admitted to communion with the church, until the church had knowledge either from himself, Barnabus, or some other, of his having obeyed the gospel in embracing the first principles of it; of which baptism is one, (Heb. 6:2). For how should they know him to be a disciple of Christ and so meet for communion with them, but by knowing that he had at least done the first things of a disciple, of which we find all along the history of the Acts of the Apostles, a being baptized, to be one, and doubtless less satisfaction would not have served them concerning him, than would concerning another disciple who had never appeared in that height of opposition against them, as he had done.

Wherein the *Objections Against this Position* viz., that None May be Regularly Admitted to the Lord's Supper, that are not First Baptized, *are Answered.*

Again, when the text tells us, that Barnabus declared unto them, how he had seen the Lord in the way, and had spoken to Him; can it be thought he could say less than what it was, that the Lord had spoke to him? And if so, then how can it be thought but that the relation of his being baptized must needs come in at his report to them inasmuch as that direction which the Lord gave Paul, about his going into a straight street in order to his further information, touching the Will of the Lord concerning him, to rehearse the carriage of Ananias towards Saul; and consequently his baptizing of him: unless it should be supposed that Barnabus made a broken and imperfect relation of the Lord's dealing with him, which we cannot do without judging Barnabus either weak or careless in that great business: for it cannot be thought that Barnabus used no more words in this relation than what are here recorded by Luke; since we have frequently, if not for the most part; but the brief heads of things recorded that were done, and spoken by Christ, the Apostles, and other disciples, John 21:25; Acts 2:40.

And we find Paul himself in making the relation of that great providence of the Lord towards him in his conversion, particularly mention his baptism, Acts 22:5-16. and that which was required of him to be found in the practice of, before he should go forth in the performance of that great work he was called unto, namely, to preach the gospel.

OBJECTION 7. It is objected, that this was in the infancy of the church, and is no binding rule to us.

ANSWER. If that be no rule to us, let it be shewn where there is another rule? besides do not all men of any understanding know, that this is the great argument brought to countenance infant baptism: and is not this the pretence by which all those traditions of men in the worship of God are brought in? How greatly is that place 1 Cor. 14:40 abused and mistaken? "Let all things be done decently and in order." From whence men take upon them to prescribe what they please, and call it order, imposing the same upon men's

Wherein the *Objections Against this Position* viz., that None May be Regularly Admitted to the Lord's Supper, that are not First Baptized, *are Answered.*

consciences, whereas order and decency there, must respect that order which he himself had prescribed in the foregoing verses, wherein is shewn, what order ought to be used in the improvement of those several gifts which God hath given to that Church in the exercise whereof the church might receive edification. They especially that are afraid to comply with the inventions of men in the worship of God in some things, should above all others be careful of bringing in any inventions of their own in other things, lest while they build again themselves the things they destroy in others; they make themselves transgressors, and give that advantage to others they would not willingly do.

OBJECTION 8. A main thing built upon, is that union with Christ gives a right to all the ordinances of Christ.

ANSWER. It is readily granted that union with Christ, signified by a visible profession of faith gives a man right to baptism, and having this union and being baptized, they have a right to church fellowship, and the Lord's Supper, etc. but that by virtue of union with Christ they have a right to the Lord's Supper; and accordingly to partake of the same before they are baptized is denied from the reasons already given, nor can it anywhere be proved.

This may be plainly illustrated by this similitude. A child, by being the eldest son of his father, has a right to his father's estate as heir thereof, as soon as his father is dead, but yet for the actual possession thereof, there is required his coming to age, till which time he cannot possess that right; the law requiring this as the order by which he is to come to the enjoyment thereof. So though union with Christ gives a man a right to all the ordinances of Christ, yet are they to be enjoyed in that order which the Law prescribeth.

OBJECTION 9. This is a dividing principle, and 'tis very censorious to judge none fit for communion in a church, but such as are baptized thereby, unchristianing all other persons that are of another mind.

Wherein the *Objections Against this Position* viz., that None May be Regularly Admitted to the Lord's Supper, that are not First Baptized, *are Answered.*

ANSWER. 1. This is no other principle but what the Scripture doth everywhere justify, as hath been largely proved before. And this objection is rather chargeable on the contrary opinion, as being that which divides the ordinance from its proper use and end by putting it out of its place, where God in His Word hath set it. There being no division made by principle, but what is made by the ignorance of the persons that oppose it about the rule and order by which Christians ought to walk; or by their willful neglect of that which is required by the Lord, of those that desire communion with the church. For if the Lord of the family prescribe an order by which it should be governed, can it be reasonable that his rule should be broken for the sake of the servant's ignorance or willfulness?

2. We censure none so rigidly as to take upon us to unchristian or unchurch them; all that we do is (in discharge of our duty to God, and faithfulness in our places) to labor to keep the Lord's ordinances (1 Cor. 11:2; Jude 3) in that purity and order the sacred records testify they were left in, and in a spirit of love and meekness to contend earnestly for the faith once delivered to the saints; which we conceive to be a duty enjoined upon all Christians, etc.

OBJECTION 10. It hath been objected from Eph. 4:4,5,6, where under the several heads there is in the fourth head one baptism. Now sayeth the objector, if we believe in the other six things there mentioned, viz., one body, one spirit, even as ye are called in one hope of your calling, one Lord, one faith, one baptism, one God and Father of all, etc., and are not found in the practice of the fourth head, viz, one baptism; what reason is there that we should be deprived of communion in the Lord's Supper for either the neglect of it, and not seeing we are bound to practice it? etc.

ANSWER. It doth appear from the text that this is a golden chain linked together by the Spirit of God Himself, the taking of one of which links away may weaken the whole: and if the wisdom of the Spirit hath linked or joined them

Wherein the *Objections Against this Position* viz., that None May be Regularly Admitted to the Lord's Supper, that are not First Baptized, *are Answered.*

together, it seems to be great presumption in any to put them assunder. Therefore let it be noted that the Apostle verse 3 exhorts the church to keep the "unity of the Spirit in the bond of peace." In the 4, 5, 6 verses, he shews, wherein the unity of the Spirit which is to be kept consists, by giving a character of the true Apostolic religion, epitomized under seven heads.

1. One God and Father of all, who is above all, and in us all.

2. One Lord the second Adam, the man Christ Jesus, by whom, and for whom are all things, the great Mediator betwixt God and man.

3. One faith, believing in this one God, and this one Lord Jesus the one Mediator.

4. One baptism, which in all the three editions thereof hath signified a profession and engagement to this one God and one Mediator by the profession of the one faith.

5. One Spirit proceeding from the Father and the Son, the great Teacher and Instructor of this one body into a further communion with the Father and the Son.

6. One body, whereof all the baptized are professed members, and whereto they are completely united by that one Spirit.

7. One hope of their calling, in believing the resurrection of the body, and eternal life, which God hath promised to all those that obey Him.

From this we may with much assurance infer, that we are under an indispensable obligation to be found in the practice of this one baptism, which holds forth our interest in, and profession of this one God and Father, one Lord Jesus Christ and one Spirit, into whose name we are commanded to be baptized, Matt. 28:19., etc. The objector supposes the bare belief (without the visible profession) of baptism, is enough; which indeed is not so: because the nature and constitution

Wherein the *Objections Against this Position* viz., that None May be Regularly Admitted to the Lord's Supper, that are not First Baptized, *are Answered*.

of this ordinance is purely practical by virtue of a positive precept, and no pretense of a speculative belief will excuse the neglect of it; any more than the neglect of an exercise of faith respecting any other of the six points, which the Holy Spirit has joined with it. (The ancients tell us the form of baptism when they expound Eph. 4:5 one law.)

QUESTION. Whereas it may be further queried whether one ordinance gives a right to the enjoyment of another?

ANSWER. It is answered, no; for we have before proved that all ordinances are to be observed in that order which the Appointer of them hath prescribed; from which we ought not to vary. For as circumcision was the first ordinance to be administered before they might be partakers of the Passover although it gave not a right to the Passover, yet might not any partake of it (before they were circumcised) without sin: so also in the New Testament baptism is the first ordinance to be administered by the direction and appointment of God, without which, the Supper of the Lord may not be received without sin. All that is pleaded for by this, is the orderly observation of the New Testament ordinances.

QUESTION. But why should any be debarred the enjoyment of those ordinances they have light into, because they want light in others?

ANSWER. It deserves to be seriously considered, whether the neglect of the ordinance of baptism doth not more arise from the want of a heart to obey God therein, by reason of the contempt put upon it, than for want of light. Is any ordinance of Jesus Christ in the New Testament more plain and clear than this? Are there not many more instances in the New Testament for the practice of this than the Lord's Supper? For besides the institution of it by Jesus Christ, instanced by the several evangelists, it is but four times mentioned, viz., Acts 2:42; 20:7; 1 Cor. 10:16; 11:23. Whereas we find besides the Commission given by Jesus Christ, Matt. 28:19, etc. that 'tis again enjoined Acts 2:38; 8:38; 10:48; 16:15, 33; 9:18; 18:8, etc. Neither do we find any one ordinance of the gospel

Wherein the *Objections Against this Position* viz., that None May be Regularly Admitted to the Lord's Supper, that are not First Baptized, *are Answered.*

so much made use of by the Apostles to incite Christians to die to sin, and live to God, as is largely demonstrated in the foregoing sheets, to which we refer, etc.

OBJECTION 11. And whereas it may be objected that 'tis love and not baptism, that discovers us to be Christ's disciples; it is answered.

ANSWER. We do readily confess that we are commanded to put on love, Col. 3:14, which is a great character of a disciple of Christ, and it is much to be lamented, that there is so little seen among saints: yet that cannot be called love, which is exercised in opposition to the order prescribed in the Word, by which ordinances ought to be administered; for as love is a grace of the Spirit of Christ; so ordinances are the appointments of the same Spirit which works grace in the hearts of Christians; all true gospel love being regulated by gospel-rule; and as all men may know the disciples of Christ by their love one to another: so also, it is a character given by the same Lord, of being a disciple when this love is manifest in keeping His commandments, John 14:15. "If ye love me keep my commandments." v. 21, "He that hath my commandments, and keepeth them, he it is that loveth me, and he that loveth me, shall be beloved of my Father, and I will love him and will manifest myself to him." verse 23. "Jesus answered and said, If any man love me, he will keep my words, and my Father will love him, and we will come unto him, and make our abode with him." verse 24, "He that loveth me not, keepeth not my sayings, and the Word which you hear is not mine, but the Father's which sent me." Now of these commandments this ordinance of baptism is not the least, and it seems to savor of little love in them that would have men believe, it is advanced in them above their brethren to charge them with want of love, as the only reason why they cannot admit persons to the Supper of the Lord, that never yet received the baptism of Christ. Therefore,

Here we can appeal to the Searcher of Hearts, that the true reason is, because we dare not break that rule and order by

Wherein the *Objections Against this Position* viz., that None May be Regularly Admitted to the Lord's Supper, that are not First Baptized, *are Answered.*

which we find the primitive saints walked, and not want of love to them. And the sense we have of the great severity God hath shewed against those that have made the least breach upon that order which He Himself hath prescribed.

These things I leave to the serious consideration of those to whom this brief essay may come, desiring they may "try all things, and hold fast that which is good."

A Biographical Sketch of William Kiffin (1616-1701)

By

John Franklin Jones

A Biographical Sketch of William Kiffin (1616-1701)

William Kiffin—Dissenter, Separatist, merchant, Particular Baptist, minister—was born in London early in 1616 of a family apparently of Welsh descent. The boy was orphaned when both parents died of the plague in June 1625. He inherited property from his father, which property relatives invested and lost in their failed business (*DNB*).

Kiffin's early attraction to biblical teachings (1631) involved attending sermons of Puritan divines (John Davenport and Lewis du Moulin) (*DNB*).

After an extended period of deep conviction, the fifteen-year-old Kiffin found solace in Christ following a sermon by John Davenport on 1 John 1:7. His faith was strengthened via a sermon by the Puritan, John Norton. Following a period of struggle with doubt, he gained assurance via the preaching of Louis du Moulin and John Goodwin (Nettles, 130).

Kiffin discovered a desire/gift for public preaching via gathering with a group of young believers who attended lectures, prayer, exhortation, testimony, and sermonizing. He increasingly became disappointed with Puritan conformity to certain Anglican rites for he found no biblical support (Nettles, 131).

Henry Jacob (1563-1624) gathered a separatist congregation in Southwark, later ministered to by John Lothrop (or

Lathrop) and Henry Jessy. Kiffin united (1638) with that congregation, where he occasionally preached (*DNB*).

This congregation had vigorously debated and been occupied with the proper subjects and proper mode of baptism for years. A group of its members had joined (1638) with John Spilsbury (1593-1662/68) in convictions against infant baptism and favoring the baptism of believers only (*TBHS* 1:231; cited in Nettles, 113, n. 2).

At 22, Kiffin united with that independent congregation in London under John Lathrop. Through his participation in discussions about baptism, he united with the newly-formed congregation of John Spilsbury (Nettles, 131).

In 1640, at 24, Kiffin led a group from that church to establish a congregation at Devonshire Square, presiding over that congregation until age eighty-six (1701) (Nettles, 132).

Kiffin early identified with Dissenter/Separatist ideas and publicly advocated the same. Ivimey called him the "father of the particular Baptists." He alone signed both the 1644 Confession and the summons (22 July 1689) calling representatives of the churches of London to a national assembly in 1689 (Nettles, 129), which assembly formulated the 1689 Confession of Faith.

He was one of four baptist disputants encountered (17 October 1642) at Southwark (*DNB*) and debated baptism with Daniel Featley (Nettles, 132). Kiffin's name leads (1644) the signatories to a confesson of faith drawn by seven churches "commonly but unjustly called anabaptists" (*DNB*).

He joined (1646) Hansard Knollys, another prominent Baptist, in a pubic disputation at Trinity Church, Coventry, with John Bryan and Obadiah Grew (*DNB*) over infant baptism (Nettles, 132).

Kiffin's dissenting ideas often brought him into conflict with the authorities, both ecclesiastical and secular. Many of those

A Biographical Sketch of William Kiffin (1616-1701)

instances involved his theological convictions. He was arrested (early 1641) at a Southwark conventicle and committed to White Lion prison, by Judge Mallet, but was released when Mallet himself was committed to the Tower in the following July (*DNB*).

Joshua Ricraft, a presbyterian merchant, attacked (1645) him as "the grand ringleader" of the baptists. Thomas Edwards (1599-1647) assailed (1646) him with holding the "atheistical" practice of unction for the recovery of the sick. Edwards rejected Kiffin's offer (15 Nov. 1644) to discus publicly the matters in Edward's church, St. Botolph's, Aldgate (*DNB*).

Kiffin was brought (12 July 1655) before Christopher Pack, lord Mayor, for preaching that infant baptism was unlawful. A heresy receiving severe penalties under the draconick ordinance of 1648, its execution upon Kiffin was postponed indefinitely. He was prosecuted (1670 & 1682) for conventicle-keeping; but was released after successfully pleading technical flaws in the charges (*DNB*).

Kiffin not only suffered personally as a dissenter, he also was an advocate for dissenting brethren. Upon the break-out of Venner's insurrection, he headed (7 Jan. 1661) a protestation of London baptists and was arrested at his meeting-house and detained in prison for four days (*DNB*).

He obtained (1673 and another occasion) interviews with the king and secured suppression of a libel against baptists and the pardon of twelve Aylesbury Baptists who had been sentenced to death (*DNB*).

Kiffin's actions included providing assylum for persecuted brethren of other lands. At the revocation of the edict of Nantes, he maintained (1685) at his own expense an exiled Huguenot family of rank (*DNB*).

His opponents brought against Kiffin charges of a political or criminal nature. A forged letter (21 December 1660) implicated him in an alleged plot following the death of the

Princess of Orange (24 December), for which he was arrested and put in the guard house, but released on 31 December (*DNB*).

At the instance of George Villiers, second duke of Buckingham, Kiffin was arrested (1664) on suspicion of involvement in an anabaptist plot against the kings's life. After an appeal in writing to Clarendon, he was released to the privy council and received no more than a threatening (*DNB*).

His house was searched (1683) on suspicion of complicity with the Rye House plot. Two of his grandsons were executed (1685) for joining the Monmouth rebellion: Benjamin Hewling was executed at Taunton on 30 September; William, at Lyme Regis on 12 September (*DNB*).

Kiffin also exhibited a wider interest in the baptists. He apparently contributed significantly to planting churches in something of a nationwide strategy and establishing communication between them and the churches in London between 1644 and 1660 (Nettles, 133). He also corresponded (1653) with the Baptists in Ireland and Wales. He participated (1675) in a scheme to provide ministerial education among the Baptists. He traveled (1676) to Wiltshire to assist in dealing with the Socinian tendencies of Thomas Collier (*DNB*).

Kiffin was a successful businessman. He began (1643) a business in woollen cloth with Holland and became wealthy and gained position via furnishing (1652) requisites for the English fleet in the Dutch war erupting in that year (*DNB*).

Kiffin held several minor positions in public and military life. He was (1647) parliamentary assessor of taxes for Middlesex. Between 1654 and 1659, he was referred to as captain and lieutenant-colonel in the London militia. He gave evidence (ca. 1663) before certain of the house of Commons and privy council against granting to a "Hamburg Company" a monopoly of woolen trade with Holland and Germany. His presentation pleased Charles II and gained him the good will of Clarendon (*DNB*).

James summoned (August 1687) Kiffin to court and included him as a London city alderman in his charter. He pled for release based on his age, his retirement from business and the death of his grandsons. He held office for the year until 21 October 1688 (*DNB*).

Kiffin died 29 December 1701 in his eighty-sixth year. He was buried in Bunhill Fields. He married Hanna in late 1634; she died 6 October 1682 at age 66. Their eldest son, William, died 31 August 1669 at age twenty. A second son, supposedly poisoned, died at Venice. A third son, Harry, died 8 December 1698, aged 44. A daughter, Priscilla, died 15 March 1679; she married Robert Liddel (*DNB*).

Kiffin's publications included the following: "A Glimpse of Sion's Glory" & c. (1641); "The Christian Man's Trials," & c. (1641); "Observations on Hosea 2:7,8" & c. (1642); "A Letter to Mr. Edwards," & c. (1644); "A Briefe Remonstrance of the ...Grounds of...Anabaptists for their Separation," & c. (1645) (answered by Ricraft in "A Looking-glass for the Anabaptists," & c. (1645); "A Declaration concerning the Publicke Dispute," & c. (1645); "A Letter to the Lord Mayor, by Lieut.-Col. Kiffin", & c. (1659); "A Sober Discourse of Right to church Communion," & c. (1681) (against open communion); prefaces to an edition of Samuel Howe's "The Sufficiency of the spirit's Teaching" & c. (1640); and the preface to "The Quakers Appeal Answered," & c. (1674) (*DNB*).

He edited, with a continuation, the "Life of Hanserd Knollys" (1692). He wrote his autobiography to 1693. That autobiography was used by Wilson in his *Dissenting Churches of London* (1808) and was edited by Orme as *Remarkable Passages in the Life of William Kiffin* (1823) (*DNB*).

SELECTED BIBLIOGRAPHY.

Dictionary of National Biography. S.v. "Kiffin, or Kiffen, William, (1616-1701)," by A[lexander] G[ordon].

Nettles, Tom. *The Baptists: Key People Involved in Forming a Baptist Identity.* Vol. 1: *Beginnings in Britain.* Geanies House, Fearn, Ross-shire, Scotland: Christian Focus Publications, 2005.

Transactions of the Baptist Historical Society. 7 vols. London: Baptist Union Publication Department, 1908-09-1920/21, 1:202-56. (TBHS).

BY JOHN FRANKLIN JONES
CORDOVA, TENNESSEE
MAY 2006

THE BAPTIST STANDARD BEARER, INC.

a non-profit, tax-exempt corporation
committed to the Publication & Preservation
of the Baptist Heritage.

CURRENT TITLES AVAILABLE IN
THE BAPTIST *DISTINCTIVES* SERIES

KIFFIN, WILLIAM — A Sober Discourse of Right to Church-Communion. Wherein is proved by Scripture, the Example of the Primitive Times, and the Practice of All that have Professed the Christian Religion: That no Unbaptized person may be Regularly admitted to the Lord's Supper. (London: George Larkin, 1681).

KINGHORN, JOSEPH — Baptism, A Term of Communion. (Norwich: Bacon, Kinnebrook, and Co., 1816)

KINGHORN, JOSEPH — A Defense of "Baptism, A Term of Communion". In Answer To Robert Hall's Reply. (Norwich: Wilkin and Youngman, 1820).

GILL, JOHN — Gospel Baptism. A Collection of Sermons, Tracts, etc., on Scriptural Authority, the Nature of the New Testament Church and the Ordinance of Baptism by John Gill. (Paris, AR: The Baptist Standard Bearer, Inc., 2006).

CARSON, ALEXANDER	Ecclesiastical Polity of the New Testament. (Dublin: William Carson, 1856).
BOOTH, ABRAHAM	A Defense of the Baptists. A Declaration and Vindication of Three Historically Distinctive Baptist Principles. Compiled and Set Forth in the Republication of Three Books. Revised edition. (Paris, AR: The Baptist Standard Bearer, Inc., 2006).
BOOTH, ABRAHAM	Paedobaptism Examined on the Principles, Concessions, and Reasonings of the Most Learned Paedobaptists. With Replies to the Arguments and Objections of Dr. Williams and Mr. Peter Edwards. 3 volumes. (London: Ebenezer Palmer, 1829).
CARROLL, B. H.	*Ecclesia* - The Church. With an Appendix. (Louisville: Baptist Book Concern, 1903).
CHRISTIAN, JOHN T.	Immersion, The Act of Christian Baptism. (Louisville: Baptist Book Concern, 1891).
FROST, J. M.	Pedobaptism: Is It From Heaven Or Of Men? (Philadelphia: American Baptist Publication Society, 1875).
FULLER, RICHARD	Baptism, and the Terms of Communion; An Argument. (Charleston, SC: Southern Baptist Publication Society, 1854).
GRAVES, J. R.	Tri-Lemma: or, Death By Three Horns. The Presbyterian General Assembly Not Able To Decide This Question: "Is Baptism In The Romish Church Valid?" 1st Edition.

	(Nashville: Southwestern Publishing House, 1861).
MELL, P.H.	Baptism In Its Mode and Subjects. (Charleston, SC: Southern Baptist Publications Society, 1853).
JETER, JEREMIAH B.	Baptist Principles Reset. Consisting of Articles on Distinctive Baptist Principles by Various Authors. With an Appendix. (Richmond: The Religious Herald Co., 1902).
PENDLETON, J.M.	Distinctive Principles of Baptists. (Philadelphia: American Baptist Publication Society, 1882).
THOMAS, JESSE B.	The Church and the Kingdom. A New Testament Study. (Louisville: Baptist Book Concern, 1914).
WALLER, JOHN L.	Open Communion Shown to be Unscriptural & Deleterious. With an introductory essay by Dr. D. R. Campbell and an Appendix. (Louisville: Baptist Book Concern, 1859).

For a complete list of current authors/titles, visit our internet site at:
www.standardbearer.org
or write us at:

he Baptist Standard Bearer, Inc.

NUMBER ONE IRON OAKS DRIVE • PARIS, ARKANSAS 72855

TEL # 479-963-3831   *FAX # 479-963-8083*
EMAIL: Baptist@centurytel.net   *http://www.standardbearer.org*

Thou hast given a standard to them that fear thee; that it may be displayed because of the truth. — Psalm 60:4

www.ingramcontent.com/pod-product-compliance
Lightning Source LLC
Chambersburg PA
CBHW032130090426
42743CB00007B/542